Vouch for This!

Vouch for This!

Defunding Private Interests, Defending Public Schools

Thomas S. Poetter
Editor

with chapters contributed by

Abayomi Samuel Abodunrin, Emmanuel Acheampong, Cerelia V. Bizzell, Carolyn S. Craig, Mastano N. W. Dzimbiri, Tahreem Fatima, Chiquita M. Hughes, Elizabeth Rae Kerr, Thomas S. Poetter, Shawnieka E. Pope, Dormetria Robinson Thompson, Dongxia Sang, Jacqlyn Schott, Hope Porta Sweeney, Jing Tan, and Tailyn Walborn

Foreword by William L. Phillis

INFORMATION AGE PUBLISHING, INC.
Charlotte, NC • www.infoagepub.com

Library of Congress Cataloging-in-Publication Data

A CIP record for this book is available from the Library of Congress
http://www.loc.gov

ISBN: 979-8-88730-441-0 (Paperback)
 979-8-88730-442-7 (Hardcover)
 979-8-88730-443-4 (E-Book)

Copyright © 2023 Information Age Publishing Inc.

All rights reserved. No part of this publication may be reproduced, stored in a retrieval system, or transmitted, in any form or by any means, electronic, mechanical, photocopying, microfilming, recording or otherwise, without written permission from the publisher.

Printed in the United States of America

Contents

Preface vii
Chiquita M. Hughes

Foreword ix
William L. Phillis

Introduction: How We Got Here xv
Thomas S. Poetter

1 **Democratic Accountability for Public Education** 1
  *Abayomi Samuel Abodunrin, Mastano N. W. Dzimbiri,
  and Emmanuel Acheampong*

2 **How Charter Schools and Universal Vouchers Recolonize
  Communities** 15
  Tahreem Fatima, Hope Porta Sweeney, and Chiquita M. Hughes

3 **Follow the Money** 49
  Tailyn Walborn, Carolyn S. Craig, and Dongxia Sang

4 **An Imminent, Hidden Tragedy** 77
  Shawnieka E. Pope, Dormetria Robinson Thompson, and Jing Tan

5 **Knowledge to Action and Manifesting (Re)Action** 97
  Cerelia V. Bizzell, Elizabeth Rae Kerr, and Jacqlyn Schott

Epilogue: A Peek at the Peak of our Pique 129
Thomas S. Poetter

Appendix A: Class Reading List 137

About the Contributors 139

Preface

Here Comes the Rain...

We were summoned, driven by intellectual curiosity and the need to frame a theoretical understanding of our personal journeys. We converged in one room, our classroom. Like droplets of water warmed by the atmosphere, we were molecules rising to a different realm of thinking. As colleagues, we transitioned together to the philosophical and practical clouds of learning, our arenas of discourse and reflection. There we used our collective power to address vouchers and charter schools, and the current and real threats they pose to equality and equity in public education.

We were intentional in transgressing boundaries and in challenging our personal narratives. We framed and reframed our thoughts. We used the past to reflect on our present. We were determined to expand our ways of knowing, to take action and advocate for public schools, one of the great public goods of our democratic republic. We were forced to wrestle with pervasive threats and ideologies—the known and unknown. Our experiences from the past spoke to our present, and we were committed to doing this work in preservation of education for the future. Layers of our consciousness were peeled back gently and sometimes abruptly. It was a process necessary for creating paths of hope—and for some, it meant healing and liberation in the moment. The past interrogated the present, and the present interrogated the future as we interrogated our lives and commitments individually and together as a team.

This book is a product of our messiness in translating our emotions, our thoughts, our passions, and purposes. We took our journey together aided by the currere process. Currere was a consuming fog and a thick shroud sometimes, bringing paralysis to some conversations but taking us down the necessary rabbit holes to clarify our purposes. This book reflects our earnest efforts to convey that which matters most to us. Even in times of dissent, we found common ground. The philosophical and practical clouds became dense. The heaviness was not melancholy, though, but rather the heaviness of responsibility and accountability for what we had learned and experienced together. And it is indicative of the critical consciousness that is part of our journey. We have been enlightened.

The result of that enlightenment is like the heat that causes the molecules of air to rise and gather in the clouds. We bring to you our collective scholarship—that which we have gathered from our experiences, molded into our research and study, and shared through the knowledge that might liberate us and others. We can no longer contain its energy and we freely release what we have gained from this encounter, because if the rain does not shower the earth, the ground becomes dry, parched. Almost all of the earth's creatures suffer in a drought, wanting relief. Just as the clouds cannot hold back the rain that revitalizes the earth, we cannot and will not hold back the collective knowledge held in these pages. For we know the power of transformation. We ourselves have been watered and fed through this process. So, we, in turn, send down the rain.

Let this work be a soaking rain.

Let this work refresh and replenish minds and hearts to seek justice, and help us all to advocate for equity for every child.

Let this knowledge and understanding be the downpours that transform the rigid, dry deaths caused by racism, classism, colonization, and neoliberalism.

Let this knowledge renew our democratic commitments to the public good of our schools, our communities, our families, and our children.

Here comes the rain.

—**Chiquita M. Hughes**

Foreword

On January 4, 2022, the Ohio Coalition for Equity and Adequacy of School Funding (the Coalition) filed a lawsuit challenging the constitutionality of the Ohio EdChoice voucher program. The public theme for the suit is "Vouchers Hurt Ohio," which is quite appropriate, descriptive of our cause, and connected to this book.

There is ample evidence that vouchers hurt public school students, voucher students attending private, voucher-receiving schools, public school districts, and Ohio taxpayers. A great deal of sound evidence of this is included in this book. The lawsuit sets forth five claims, all of which the trial court judge allowed to go forward to trial when the State Defendants' Motion to Dismiss was rejected.

Before enumerating and discussing the five claims, a review of Ohio's path from a somewhat innocuous pilot project specific to the Cleveland School District to universal vouchers is warranted. The seeds for the Cleveland voucher venture were planted by President George H. W. Bush (Bush 41) on November 25, 1991, at the behest of Ohio Governor George Voinovich, when speaking to a large gathering of citizens, including a substantial number of teachers, school administrators, and political leaders.

The pivotal point of the Bush 41 speech on that fateful voucher seeding day was that every public school student should be provided a voucher, an idea at that time not well-received by Ohioans. Governor Voinovich's response to the public criticism of the voucher idea was that the matter

---

Vouch for This!, pages ix–xiii
Copyright © 2023 by Information Age Publishing
www.infoagepub.com
All rights of reproduction in any form reserved.

should be studied; hence, he appointed a commission to investigate the matter. Voinovich appointed a campaign supporter—Akron, Ohio, Industrialist David Brennan—as chair of the commission. Brennan was known as a school privatization advocate.

The commission recommended that every Ohio school district provide vouchers to students. This was not a popular recommendation, but Voinovich and Brennan proceeded with their voucher crusade. The legislature, upon the recommendation of the governor, targeted the academically beleaguered Cleveland School District for a voucher pilot project.

The maiden voucher project in Cleveland was funded by monies within the Cleveland School District budget and provided vouchers, coincidentally, in the same number as the available empty seats in the parochial system in Cleveland. From that humble beginning, fueled with the rhetoric of saving children from "failing school districts," Ohio, as of July 1, 2023, has a universal voucher system wherein even billionaires can be awarded vouchers backed by public funds to pay private school tuition.

Here are the claims that the plaintiffs, backed by over 100 Ohio public school districts, set forth in the lawsuit:

Count 1

The creation of one or more systems of uncommon schools is unconstitutional. Funding for the EdChoice private school voucher program comes from the same line-item in the two-year state budget that funds public schools. Each public tax dollar that goes to private schools is a dollar less for public schools. That's unconstitutional.

Count 2

Lawmakers have failed to adequately fund a thorough and efficient system. Private school vouchers force local school districts to raise local taxes through levies to make up the reduction in state dollars. That's unconstitutional.

Count 3

Private school vouchers make segregation in public schools worse. Private schools take public tax dollars while applying litmus tests to pick and choose their students based on academics, athletics, disciplinary records, financial status, race, and religion. That's unconstitutional.

Count 4

No religious or other sect shall ever have any exclusive right to or control of any part of the school funds of the state. It's there in black and white in the Ohio Constitution. More than 90 percent of private schools in Ohio are parochial with hundreds of millions of dollars going to sectarian schools. That's unconstitutional.

Count 5
Ohio citizens hold all political power under the Ohio Constitution. When the court rules EdChoice vouchers unconstitutional, state lawmakers will no longer be permitted to fund the EdChoice voucher program. The EdChoice private school voucher program on the face is unconstitutional.

Ohio's political representation in the legislature is lopsided due to the gerrymandered legislative boundaries. Those in power, particularly in the Ohio Senate, have been focused on legislating universal vouchers for about 15 years. Legislators ignore the views of voucher opponents in legislative hearings, community meetings, and private conversation; therefore, an appeal to the judiciary is the only option available to voucher opponents.

The Ohio Coalition for Equity and Adequacy of School Funding is committed to winning in the court of law. It is equally committed to winning in the court of public opinion.

The citizens of no state in the Union have, in a statewide vote, approved vouchers. State legislators throughout the nation are typically out of sync with citizens regarding this issue. However, Ohioans have not been given the opportunity to vote on the voucher issue. Neither has this issue been sufficiently vetted in public discourse.

When the EdChoice voucher debate catches the full attention of Ohioans, the voucher movement may be curtailed or brought to an end due to public pressure on state officials. To this end, efforts like this book by Thomas Poetter and his students, *Voucher for This! Defunding Private Interest, Defending Public Schools,* may help the efforts to roll back the gains made to embed the voucher program in the state's policy apparatus, budget, and practices. The work has the potential of sparking a robust public discourse on school privatization.

The book deals with both charter schools and vouchers, whereas the current litigation is confined to the voucher issue; however, the charter school industry is ripe for a court challenge, as well.

This book is honed in on the communication of the efficacy of public education and the flaws inherent in privatized alternatives—vouchers and charters; Policy scholarship and analysis of educational movements is a key tool that the Coalition and citizens from all walks of life can use in winning in the court of public opinion. Many citizens and even many directly involved with the public common school system are not conversant with the ideas and practices of democratic accountability inherent in authentic public education as discussed in the opening of Chapter 1.

Chapter 1 details the undemocratic practices that have emerged in the U.S. education system as a result of the ongoing expansion of voucher programs and charter schools. Further in Chapter 1, it is emphatically stated that "democratic accountability lies at the heart of any functioning democracy ensuring that power remains vested in the hands of the people."

Article 1, section 2 of the Ohio Constitution states, "All political power is inherent in the people." This is an important message the Coalition is attempting to convey to the court and public, and one in which the actions suggested in Chapter 5 can help the Coalition win in the court of public opinion.

The segregating effect of vouchers is an essential message the Coalition has been forwarding for some time. Chapter 2 reinforces that argument: Privatized alternatives to the common school system contribute to tribalism. This coincides with the message from the Coalition to the court and the general public.

Chapter 3 provides a discussion of the funding of the public common school system and how charters and vouchers detract from it. These alternatives remove funds from the public common schools. The conclusion of this chapter—"What we are saying is that our tax dollars are public funds and should not be used for private enterprise"—perfectly aligns with the Coalition's view.

Chapter 4 examines the false hopes of the voucher movement. This is a central, compelling reason to have the EdChoice voucher scheme declared unconstitutional.

Chapter 5 provides some powerful action items that the Coalition could use in winning in the court of public opinion. It responds to the question of "So what?" regarding the problems identified in the first four chapters. This chapter presents the need to counter the voucher movement and suggests some public actions going forward. The Coalition welcomes the advocacy inherent in Chapter 5.

We hope that many will read this book and support efforts to roll back the gains that have been made to privatize education in Ohio and beyond. We know that much is at stake as new policies and budgets take root. It's time for scholars and activists, politicians and citizens, to stand up for public school policies that benefit all students and build strong school systems throughout Ohio and other states that all students can access and excel in. Nothing is fairer, more just, or equitable than that, and indicative of our great democratic republic's important role in building a well-educated, informed, and politically active populace.

—**William L. Phillis**, Executive Director
Ohio Coalition for Equity and Adequacy of School Funding

Introduction

How We Got Here

In the Fall of 2022, I was already thinking about the Summer of 2023. I would be leaving my role as department chair after a five-year term on June 30, 2023, and entering a semester of faculty leave to retool as I made my way back to full time teaching and scholarship. Administration, especially through the pandemic, had taken a toll on me. Maybe being department chair would have taken that toll on me anyway—no matter the five-year period over my nearly 30 years now in higher education. But I just can't imagine continuing to face the mounting issues with colleagues over flailing budgets, labor unrest, post-pandemic issues of all kinds, and everything else under the sun that is plaguing higher education writ large and right here in my own backyard at Miami from the perspective of mid-management.

I was happy to be walking away from the chair role and back to faculty, in the coming summer of 2023, with no complicated, pressing things to plan or do before a needed break from the fray, on my way back to teaching and working with students full-time.

But then Jing Tan, one of our all-time greatest doctoral students and co-author of this text—among so many over the years including all of the authors of this book—walked into my office, sat down for our scheduled meeting to discuss a myriad of projects she had been helping me with, and said, "You know, Dr. Poetter, you promised me several years ago that before I graduated you would teach a knowledge production class where students write a book with you, and I have never had a chance to do that because you have been chair this whole time. Is that going to happen? Time is running out…."

I laughed nervously, cornered again, and said, "Jing, that really hurts. I would love to do that, but the last chance I would have to do it is next summer and while Summer 2023 scheduling is coming up, there is no guarantee the faculty will even let me do it, and I was thinking about fading out a bit when this job ends next June, not ramping anything new up. So, I don't think it's going to happen."

Grim silence. I had never seen Jing Tan crestfallen. Literally, nearly every drop of energy and life went out of her. And that's not Jing Tan. I could tell by her expression that she didn't appreciate that I had laughed. She thought I didn't want to do a book project *with her*. Not true, but I could see where she was coming from. I didn't want to be the kind of professor/colleague who breaks promises. I felt horrible, and folded. Plus, this is the kind of work I hadn't been able to do for so long and wanted to get back to as soon as possible… I decided on the spot to jump back in.

"Okay, I can see if I can get an elective course on the summer schedule but there are no guarantees." She came alive and as alert as ever in the next breath and I wondered, "Have I been had?" But to this day, I continue to revel in the sincerity of Jing Tan, her purity of spirit, her deep intellectual interests, and her energy. She wanted to take a course with me where students address a critical issue in education and write a flash book about it in 100 days.

You're reading this book, at least in part, because of Jing Tan and her tenacity of spirit, her energy, and my penchant for not breaking promises, if I can help it!

A few minutes later, thinking out loud with Jing about potential special topics for the course if it somehow came to be, I mentioned my interest for addressing—through scholarship and public action like writing a book with students—the movement in the nation and the state of Ohio to universalize school vouchers, mainly to feed the education system that is becoming so heavily more privatized, especially through the charter school movement. I expressed my framing for what I thought was happening—that private interests would ultimately trump the public good—and for the kind of course we could have in the summer to help students learn how to create public knowledge about a topic of interest and importance to the field and to citizens of all stripes.

She liked the idea. She thought we could recruit a class, and she volunteered to help with that. And ultimately after a few months of planning, getting the course on schedule, and students registering for it, the class happened in the summer session of 2023. This book is the work of that 15-person team, and their professor.

A Track Record With Student Projects

As I met students such as Jing over the years in courses and as an advisor, I shared examples of work that our students had published as a result of projects they engaged during coursework with me that had been collaboratively produced, typically, and usually the centerpiece of the curriculum and pedagogy of the course. Over the past 25 years I have written extensively about my thinking behind this type of teaching and how I do knowledge production projects with students (Poetter et al., 1997; Poetter, 2010; Poetter & Googins, 2015; Poetter, 2016; Poetter, 2020).

The project that started all of this happened with my first class of student teaching interns at Trinity University in San Antonio in 1994, whom I challenged to conduct action research projects on their journeys as beginning teachers, and to publish a book about their work. That book, *Voices of Inquiry in Teacher Education* (Poetter et al., 1997), cemented my interest in doing this type of study, knowledge production, and at times educational activism with students, and proved to be my own "proof of concept" experience for how this work is both curricular and pedagogical.

The last project I did with doctoral students that used a similar approach to framing the course that produced this book happened in the Summer of 2015. That class wrote *Was Someone Mean to You Today? The Impact of Standardization, Corporatization, and High Stakes Testing on Students, Teachers, Communities, Schools, and Democracy* (Poetter & Googins, 2015), which addressed the curriculum standardization movement and how the state—through all manner of powerful but ill-advised, ineffective approaches including high stakes testing regimes—had been putting the curriculum, and as a result, teaching itself, in jeopardy. That powerful process to limit classroom freedom through standardization over many years had taken a toll on all of us as educators, but especially on students in classrooms. That movement had to be challenged; I made no bones about it: the course would be focused on producing scholarship that advocates for policy change.

What We Did in This Course

The approach I used in the 2015 class for taking on the testing movement mirrors the one that we engaged for this class project. I asked students to study the topic with me over the course of a six-week period and seeded the course discussion with 11 items of scholarship about the topic and the approaches to the course. That list of required pre-readings grew to 16 shared items and is included here in Appendix A as a reference list. I wanted the students to read several common items to put them together in conversation with the topic and approaches to the course that were accessible, mostly short, and solid pieces. Most of the items were critical of the voucher and the charter and education privatization movements taking shape to benefit from the expansion of vouchers across the union and especially in Ohio, our home state, and home of Miami University.

Here's what I said to prospective students in my early email advertising the course in December 2022:

> My intent for this summer elective, beginning the week after graduation, May 17 through June 21 (6 weeks), is to recruit all comers to work on this next project, based loosely (so far) on the following topic: The threats to public education and democracy posed by the voucher and charter school movements in Ohio and United States. My plan is to use the currere approach as our research methodology, to read and write and share ideas together, to produce text, and to mold it into a book-length work. Almost all of this would happen during the six weeks of the course. Some finishing duties may fall to a few after the course is completed.

Fifteen students signed up for the elective course!

As I put the course together, I wanted the students to consume the perspectives of scholars, and scholars of color in particular, who were at least skeptical of the ideas and practices surrounding the rise of charter schools and the vouchers being subsidized by states with public money to fund privatizing entities like many charters are, and now, coming full steam ahead with plans for vouchers to be used by families to fund private school tuition and homeschooling costs. Though vouchers have been around a long time, the key difference now is their continued expansion, in some cases becoming universal. And so, we read Sanders, Stovall, and White's (2018) book *Twenty-First Century Jim Crow Schools: The Impact of Charters on Public Education*, which, along with the other pre-readings, created a good amount of feedback and fervor in the class, as well as grounding knowledge from a race-conscious perspective for how the movements were having a profoundly negative impact on public education.

To be clear, I made no effort for the most part from the beginning, during, or even now after the course with our students, to uncouple the notions and practices around school vouchers and charter schools. The reason for that decision is that I see vouchers and charters as aspects/manifestations of the privatization movement in our society and in education, being led mainly by politicians and business people to disestablish and defund public education by positioning the public schools pejoratively as "government schools" that are merely practicing social and academic indoctrination, and to get a piece of the education money pie into the hands of private providers since so much of our public money, they say, is being wasted on a government monopoly of schooling that is overfunded, inefficient, and driven by selfish labor, aka teachers unions (Welner, Orfield, & Huerta, 2023).

I don't agree with any of that, find the entire trope disingenuous, and believe that those who do agree with it and make things happen for the voucher and charter movements politically in our statehouses and in the new private charter schools popping up all over our state and country are driven by a certain recipe combining politics and greed:

- The proponents are not well-intentioned, and often say they are, but mainly seek to benefit, primarily through monetary profit, by defunding our system of public schooling in our state and across the country by moving public money out of legitimate public schools and into mostly illegitimate, inexperienced, and unaccountable private hands.
- They do not seek equity, but say they do and change their tune when conditions change, the market doesn't pan out, or the money and students literally lead elsewhere.
- They do not seek efficiency, but say they do and manifest that "commitment" by cutting costs on teaching and other resources to make a profit, not to serve students better.
- They do not seek greater student achievement, but say they do and employ the means to do so, including draconian ones, that repeat educational harms already happening to so many students in schools across the land.

What is different or transformational or better about any of that? Nothing.

As a base for proceeding—which I hope to have been modeling so far in my writing here—I wanted students to learn about a movement in the curriculum studies field called "currere," which is a personal, autobiographical approach to scholarship that seeks to attend to the question, "What has been and is my journey in education?" (Pinar, 1994). Currere is "...a four-step process that involves viewing life experience and our interpretations of reality as a venture into curriculum theorizing, that is 'the scholarly effort to understand the curriculum, conceived... as complicated conversation'" (Pinar, 2012, p. 1).

I want students to understand and then operationalize in their own work that educational issues are complicated and political, and that scholarship is never neutral, even if it claims to be! So, foregrounding a personal, autobiographical perspective in academic work in education claims a ground for taking steps forward that recognize the value of personal experience, that puts human life forward as valuable and telling and educational in and of itself, and that brings the scholar closer to a point of view and the phenomenon at hand, not more distant from a position or in a seemingly more appealingly objective, safe, and authoritative space from which to do the work. Currere, instead, helps the curriculum policy scholar see the connections among past, present, and future experiences and perhaps to discern a way forward from both a personal and a deeply systemic point of view that can lead to outcomes that are just, equitable, and build on human possibility, not tear it down.

One of the things I am committed to as a professor is helping students find their voices as academics, to helping them move past thinking of academic and educational policy work as bland, only technical, merely in some indisputable way as scientific. Again, not possible. Curriculum policy work is human work. It is discerning, interpretive work. It involves determining and making choices and taking value positions, like everything else in education does. Our work isn't always somehow stronger or more legitimate by default because it is more scientific or science-y (by the way, there is really nothing wrong with science except when it is posed as the only thing that is right), with proofs that can be established, or laws of action and behavior found and proven, with findings that are unassailable and mathematically indisputable (this rarely happens anyway and also may be impossible!). The best education scholarship, from my point of view, tells a story, lays out a defensible position, seeks movement and buy-in and legitimate support for reasons that hopefully lead to the strengthening of our educational system, to the enhancing of individual outcomes in education, and to the building of lives together across boundaries of all sorts that help us create a stronger, more unified and democratic republic together regardless of our differences. None of these things are possible without sacrifices, compromises, and learning. Currere helps us frame the work on this type of journey.

In addition to using currere, I also made the case with students early in the course that I wanted them to participate in what scholarly policy entities call "advocacy scholarship," which we would claim that those behind the voucher and charter movements themselves have been creating and participating in from the very beginning, from their own political and economic agenda perspectives even though they may not define their work as policy advocacy. We adopted the definition that "(p)olicy advocacy is the process of negotiating and mediating a dialogue through which influential networks, opinion leaders, and ultimately, decision-makers take ownership of your ideas, evidence, and proposals, and subsequently act upon them" (Young & Quinn, 2012, p. 26).

Our approach, in particular with this book project then, was to make an attempt at engaging in "*a deliberate process of persuasive communication*—in all activities and communication tools" in which "advocates are trying to get the target audiences to understand, be convinced, and take ownership of the ideas presented. Ultimately, they should feel the urgency to take action based on the arguments presented" (Young & Quinn, 2012, p. 26). Our hope is that this work is persuasive, that groups of citizens and activists will read it, and perhaps that politicians will reconsider their quick and misinformed decisions to defund (not defend!) public education. Only the readers and the public can be effective purveyors of movement in this direction; we are glad for opportunities to support that work, and would wholeheartedly join in. We support the notion of "transfer of ownership of core ideas and thinking. In essence, this implies preparing decision makers and opinion leaders for the next policy window or even pushing them to open one in order to take action. If advocates do their job well, decision makers will take the ideas that have been put forward and make changes to the current policy approach in line with that thinking" (p. 26). Only time will tell if our work has its intended impact, and time is growing short. Let's hope it doesn't run out…

Over the course of the class meetings in Summer of 2023, we engaged each other in common readings and discussions, charted directions in our thinking together, planned how to organize our writing, surfaced what I call "bits" and "fragments" and "treatments" as writing teams, and constructed this narrative.

In the next sections of this introduction, I describe what I mean by bits and fragments and treatments and how the students used them to build their advocacy chapters. Then, I lay out what our class members thought was essential background for any reader of this book, especially someone just looking to learn about what the controversy around the movement toward vouchers and charters in our education systems is all about: that is, a short explanation about what vouchers and charters are with simplified descriptions given all that is happening and what is at stake. I conclude this introductory chapter with a few descriptive sentences about the book body's five chapters.

"Bits and Fragments and Treatments... Oh My!"

After we were settled into the class and began working on the pre-reading list together in discussions, I asked students to create autobiographical "bits or fragments," or short, sticky stories told from a first-person perspective to highlight and interrogate their own understanding of and connection to the charter and voucher movements. They could start with a story framing their own educational experience and background if they liked, but if the story overlapped with the themes and ideas and possibilities in our pre-reading list, that would be great! The goal would be to use the bits to frame the important points they wanted to make about vouchers and charters—and, overall, the privatization movements in education—in order to set up their treatments of their points. Treatments are the analyses that follow the data, an effort to expand and interrogate and reframe the main points with other scholarship and evidence (Poetter & Googins, 2015).

I also encouraged the class to think about writing interludes, too, which I define as creative ways of connecting their fragments of experience and their emerging understanding of the complicated morass surrounding the privatization movements in education writ large to the larger points at hand. The point of all of these steps is to address the issues at hand from multiple viewpoints, to dive deeply into the nuanced ways that we can discuss what's at stake with our readers, and in the end perhaps suggest reasoned, even inspiring ways forward.

Once we were several class sessions into the course and becoming comfortable as a team and our discussions were taking shape, I asked the students to engage in a planning exercise involving an adaptation of "open space technology" (Owen, 2008). Open Space Technology is an approach to collaborative agenda setting which was designed mainly for organizations to utilize their own talent to create agendas for professional education and development, especially in larger, face-to-face meeting situations. My truncated, adapted version of this approach for making complicated, usually difficult decisions collaboratively with new groups of scholar-authors is to ask members to consider what they would be willing to work on for a chapter in the book, to name it, and to define it on one piece of chart paper in front of the whole team. The process of surfacing their potential chapter ideas took about an hour, and then we spent another good hour in discussions about each of the eight ideas represented by each of the eight or so persons and the chart paper starter activity.

I published the charts about the ideas for chapters for everyone to look at over the weekend and at our next session we began to edit and shape potential chapter titles and focuses from the charts. Then students self-selected into chapter teams, balancing them at three members each for the five chapters included here. My thinking on these limits was that the groups should be balanced in numbers (three persons on each of five teams) to equally distribute the labor and support needed to craft each of the chapters in the remaining time in the course. And I made a judgment that eight chapters just felt too long with the potential that the chapters would come-in too thin and under-resourced. The class navigated this process with great skill, and with the relational acumen that I would expect of advanced students. But this isn't easy work, and after I mentioned that I thought that in a very exciting and energizing period of engagement during the open space exercise that we had several instances of some class members talking over others, the students themselves suggested that we come up with new norms for the group to avoid any further incidences of that:

Class Norms for Complicated Conversations

1. There's only 1 microphone: One person speaks at a time
2. Be open-minded.
3. Practice active listening.
4. Assume that classmates have the best of intentions.
5. We are all on the same team!

And as the commonly produced items kept building up in the course such as the pictures of the charts, the norms, the chapter titles and outlines, etc., even I realized that the documents couldn't merely be flying around through email or housed in the hard-to-access canvas platform course files. So, Jacqlyn took initiative to create a shared google drive for each of the chapter teams to house their work taking shape, especially the chapter drafts. That worked very well and I'm grateful for the students' leadership and support with that move. Thanks, Jacqlyn.

Near the end of the course, as drafts of the chapters were taking shape, the Chapter 5 team—which viewed its work as helping to summarize many of the movements in the book into suggested ways forward for readers—requested that we set a deadline for chapter drafts that would allow them to read them ahead of the next class session and to meet and discuss their findings and ideas with the other chapter teams face-to-face. I think this step helped us coalesce, gel, pull some outlying ideas and possibilities together, and get a sense of the progress we were making and the momentum we had. It's hard to see things coming together if you can't see them coming together! This is another example of outstanding student leadership in the course.

Our final class meeting became the due date for the chapter drafts, and that night we had a potluck dinner and a conversation about the course, what was learned, and how to proceed. In that meeting, we created a schedule for the finishing work that happens with books: putting the front matter together, recruiting writers for a Foreword and Preface (Chiquita's ideas expressed at our first session became the Preface!), setting a timeline for a final reading of the finished drafts by all of the authors, etc. And, in the end, the students reiterated to me, "We sure hope that you can lay out some of the common ground that readers will need to understand where we are coming from, what we have learned about these movements, what's happening and what's at stake."

What's Happening and What's at Stake

I think it's important before I lay out what I understand to be the general state of the situation regarding the privatization efforts in our nation with regards to charter schools and vouchers, in particular, that I make a few facts in terms of my own perspective crystal clear to the reader. In the main, it's important to know that I am a public schooling advocate in my life and work but also that I have benefited immensely from private education experiences. In addition, while I am critical about the role of many politicians and most capitalists with a neoliberal orientation to seek out markets to exploit; to displace families and students; to make promises they can't keep regarding equity and services and student achievement; to flatten the well-being of teachers and their families by lowering salaries and benefits; and to undervalue the importance of teacher education, certification, and ongoing teacher development—among several other critical aspects of their paths leading to demise: I have nothing against private education whatsoever. In fact, I think it has an important place, and should maintain it, in the U.S. educational landscape.

As a child, I went to a small public elementary school in a community that valued education (Bunker Hill Elementary School, St. Marys, Ohio; see Poetter, 1994). Several of my childhood friends went to a small, private Catholic school in our town through grade 8, but then they joined the rest of us in high school (my graduating class was 1981). There were no other regional, private school competitors for high school students in my hometown during my youth. Students generally graduated from high school in my town (St. Marys Memorial High School, well over 90%), and many went to college and others into the trades, technical education programs, the military, and/or work.

I went to a small, private liberal arts college affiliated with a mainline protestant denomination (Heidelberg College, The United Church of Christ, 1985) and studied English and Business and played college sports. I could make the teams at The Berg, an NCAA Division III school, and benefited immensely over the years from the community of scholars I grew with—professors, classmates, and teammates. After college, I went straight into a private university's master's program for students intending on going into the protestant ministry (Princeton Theological Seminary, Presbyterian Church USA, 1988; see Poetter, 2003). During that time in seminary, I decided to go into teaching instead of the formal ministry, having caught the bug for working with students after landing athletic coaching jobs in the local public high school, and subsequently earning a public school teaching certificate through Princeton University in New Jersey in one of the first "back door" certificate granting programs in the nation.

After seminary, thinking I would find a teaching job in a public school district in the summer of 1988 in the Midwest, the market was full of baby boom teachers in their prime, and I couldn't find an opening I could win (those failed interview experiences make for some good stories), even with my resume. However, late that summer I landed a private high school teaching, athletic coaching, and assistant chaplaincy position in Indiana (Culver Academies, a non-sectarian, independent school, 1988–1991). Culver is where I cut my teeth in the classroom, learned about students and classroom life, and became the teacher I am now. I left the classroom and the basketball court and pulpit for Indiana University (1994), one of the great public universities in the western hemisphere, to study for my PhD in Curriculum & Instruction, and took my first teaching position at Trinity University in San Antonio (1994–1997), a private, regional university, where I worked in an urban public high school partnership supporting teaching interns in the university's post baccalaureate master's program for teacher certification and teacher education. I came home to Ohio's public higher education system to a position at Miami University (1997-present), where I have spent the balance of my career in higher education.

So, as you can see, my life in education has been diverse in terms of the public/private equation, and I have gained much from my educational experiences, the learning, the relationships, and the attending associations that have accrued to me have had great value. They represent, in many ways, the diversity of public/private opportunities in the education domain available to many but not necessarily accessible by all. But from the beginning I have had and have continued to develop a sense of how immensely important our public education institutions are for the well-being of the republic, in particular the role they play in helping us develop a diverse, unified, knowledgeable citizenry and electorate. I was able to pay for my private education experiences, beyond the taxes my family and I paid and the lower salaries available in the private school jobs I took at the secondary and higher education levels, and think that others should pay their own way through the system if they choose the private route, as well. Unfortunately, this set of values has largely been rejected by many and the actual flow of public money has become steadily more likely to wind up in the hands of privateers and those who can already afford the costs of private education.

Therefore, given my own personal background and the up-close experiences of learning about the various movements in play, I want to frame how the charter school and voucher movements—which, in my view, are mainly driven by powerful neoliberal ideas and focus on privatization—play a role in the educational offerings of students today, and what's at stake for the students, communities, and for all of us when families face the complicated choices they have to make about schooling. As an introduction here, I take a view from several thousand feet up, given that the details are often stunningly and devilishly complicated on the ground.

First, it is important to build on my previous personal story that lays out my own journey through public and private education opportunities available to many. I want to reiterate that there is nothing wrong, at root, with private education. In fact, historians acknowledge that the Catholic system of private schools in the nation, for instance, emerged from a lack of religious tolerance for Catholicism in the public sphere, including education, which was dominated by protestant, middle class values and practices (Tyack, 1974; Kaestle, 1983). Many private schools, as a result, in the United States are sectarian, or parochial, like Catholic schools: That is, they are tied to an affiliated, religious denomination.

There are also private, non-sectarian, independent schools that may have an organizing focus (a military academy, or a performing arts school, for example) but no affiliation with a religious organization. Our system of public and private education options has basically thrived through the inception of the common school and over our vastly complicated 250 history, though there have been extremely difficult periods of the journey, including our road toward desegregation, which continues to be long and perilous (Anderson, 1995; Siddle Walker, 1996). Though these private education options are extremely diverse, they are also typically out of reach for many families due to cost and sometimes distance, and were often created, frankly, and especially in the past 70 years, to support White flight and segregation (Suitts, 2023). However, the choice movements that include various forms of vouchers for education expenses make it possible for more families than ever to access public funds to pay for private education, and even for those who never attended public schools or who don't need the money in the first place. This became possible (though perhaps not fully "legal" even at the time) in areas of the American South after Brown v. Board of Education in the 1950s and the Civil Rights Bills of the 1960s (Suitts, 2023), then it has become fully legalized in recent years through shifts and expansions in voucher laws across the nation, state by state, in the past several decades (Welner, Orfield, & Huerta, 2023).

Second, one important aspect for understanding how complicated all of this can be, is that the charter school movement—which has public and private aspects and manifestations to it—was born out of early interests expressed with public action mainly by educational progressives, who hoped to establish small, public schools that were often designed to serve low-income students of color, for instance, and to create opportunities for students who needed support beyond what traditional public schools could typically provide, such as a more challenging, less rote curriculum; alternative teaching approaches designed to meet students' interests; and often small school size or class size settings. Many citizens support these ideas across the political spectrum, but the grassroots, equity-oriented, even progressive movements that dotted the landscape in the 1980s and 1990s and earlier were soon co-opted or surpassed by the larger, corporate movements by states and municipalities and corporate groups by the early 2000s (Gregory & Smith, 1987; Gregory, 1993; Newmann & Wehlage, 1995; Sizer, 1997; Fabricant & Fine, 2012).

Third, as charter schools began to emerge significantly by the turn of the 21st century, they were mainly founded as public charters, which were typically attached to public school districts and allowed to operate with far fewer of the educational and financial accountability measures that often strangle the educational life out of public school students and personnel (Poetter & Googins, 2015). In fact, these "public charter schools" were and still are officially called "community schools" in Ohio. Many school districts had already been experimenting with their own choice programs, offering schools-within-schools and magnet schools and other alternative school programs as options for public school parents. But many of those public options were co-opted and often overshadowed as public charter schools took shape and found success, and as private education companies began to emerge and make in-roads as they responded to tragedies (see New Orleans, for instance—in the wake of Hurricane Katrina—Chicago, and New York City, as noted in Sanders, Stovall, and White, 2018) and learned the lessons necessary to thrive in the educational and political environments emerging in real time.

Truth be told, private education enterprises met the markets where they were—that is, at places in which public opinion and personal experiences with education, especially in urban public school districts, had become more negative than positive—making it possible for states to pass voucher laws, to create funding streams for "public" charter schools (often run by private entities and receiving public money to operate, as in Ohio), and create the legal openings and legitimate pathways for private companies to develop schools/school programs, market them to chartering entities, and get their foot in the door. Once that happened, the political will accrued by increasingly right-leaning state houses, including Ohio's, which have been led by Republicans since 2010 and now hold a supermajority across the all branches of government, pushed voucher laws past their experimental phases and into full-blown programs that may result in universal voucher programs as we speak: meaning, in "backpack bills," where state education appropriations per pupil follow the student—with little if any regulation—so families can spend on education expenses regardless of their circumstances. Full voucher funding soon could become the rule, not the exception. (Note: Ohio's governor signed a new budget in July 2023 that includes a universal voucher appropriation for nearly $1 billion per year; see Shimp, Vorys, & O'Donnell, 2023).

As Welner, Orfield, and Huerta (2023) explain, research long-term indicates that once funding streams are developed in education, those few receiving the benefits of them "are much more deeply impacted by the policy than are the dispersed population of taxpayers footing the bill, so those parents and private schools tend to form organizations that become a political force protecting and trying to expand the programs" (p. 4). Once citizens and private companies get their foot in the door, they become extremely difficult to dislodge, all the while most of the population is indifferent or unaware of the changing political and economic landscape caving in on them. Often, as is the case of the ever-expanding pool of the public's tax money flowing to education vouchers: as one powerful political and economic position expands, another diminishes.

Fourth, the chum in the water, then, is the confluence of the increased *opportunity* to access public money for private gain (for companies and customers both!), along with private education companies proving to be incredibly able to quickly offer expanded *program development* of their prospective services to school districts and to communities. All participants have the goal of gobbling up "their share." That's how capitalism driven by neoliberal values works. So, politicians and governments expand the percentage of tax dollars they are willing to spend on charter and voucher programs, whose dollars will mostly flow to education companies that run charter schools, and to the private entities that own and run their own charter school or network of schools, and to homeschooling families and students who have never attended public schools but whose parents qualify for vouchers to pay for private school tuition.

And governments have made the options very easy and manageable, including: creating direct payment voucher schemes where the state sends money directly to private schools, sometimes at rates double the amount or more that the state would have sent to a public school to support a student (Dyer & Reedy, 2022); tax free education savings plans that can be used for private school expenses; and tax credit schemes that can heavily reduce tuition payments by reducing individual tax liability (Garcia & Steele, 2023); and generous per pupil allocations directly from state coffers to fund public and private entities running public charter schools (Shimp, Vorys, & O'Donnell, 2023).

It's important to clarify here: Most of the money already flowing to charters in Ohio, for instance, has been public money that would have been appropriated to traditional public schools. Districts in Ohio, for instance, lost money in the recent past that would have been appropriated to them and it was sent directly to the new school, typically a chartered school run by a private organization. So, I have to clarify that the term I am using mostly throughout this chapter is private charter schools, though national entities continue to refer to themselves as public charter schools because they are receiving public monies to operate. These charters, though, are essentially private entities that don't have to follow the same rules that public schools do though they are receiving public tax money to operate. And, they are mostly run by private corporations.

The National Alliance for Public Charter Schools states that 65% of charter schools are "freestanding," that is that they seek authorization for the charter from a chartering entity and then run the school and financial aspects of it, including governance, on their own (White & Xu, 2022). As Sanders, Stovall, and White (2018) note, two types of private management structures are creating and running private charter schools or networks: Education Management Organizations (EMOs), which manage for-profit education providers without full executive authority, typically; and Charter Management Organizations (CMOs), which manage networks of private charter schools but are non-profit entities (pp. 73–74).

> The National Alliance considers an organization to be a management organization if it: (1) manages at least three schools, (2) serves a minimum of 300 students, and (3) is a business entity separate from the schools it manages. The two types of management organizations are charter management

organizations (CMOs) and education management organizations (EMOs). **CMOs account for 26% of charter schools nationwide, while EMOs manage 9% of charter schools.** (authors' bolded text, White & Xu, 2022)

Fifth, for me, regardless of the difficulties presented by recent Supreme Court cases, like *Zelman* (2002), which "cleared away the establishment clause barrier to voucher growth"; *Espinoza* (2020), which "equated separation-of-church-and-state arguments to antireligious discrimination under the Free Exercise Clause, holding that states cannot deny funding to religious schools because of their religious status"; and *Carson* (2022), which "extended Espinoza to denial of funding because of the religious uses of that funding," the fact that public money is flowing to private entities rankles, and suggests a shift from viewing vouchers as taboo in the 1970s to nearly constitutionally required today (Welner, Orfield, & Huerta, 2023, p. 9). This framing suggests that while the law shifts, maybe what is at stake doesn't shift, like the questions that persisted in our class and individually, that need to be addressed, such as:

What becomes of our way of life, our democratic republic, the substance of it, like who we view ourselves to be together as a nation-state, not just as individuals...

- When we create seemingly parallel systems of education that overwhelmingly advance the segregation of students of color and those who are low-income from the rest, driving us further in distance away from each other's lives, both literally and figuratively?
- When we establish rules of action (or none!) so dissimilar to each other, like the fact that accountability rules for measuring student achievement and monitoring the expenditure of funding are not the same for all entities funded by public monies?
- When we create school opportunities for students that don't have the baseline protections we demand for every student in traditional public schools built into the school program?
- When our scholarly colleagues who are supposedly "objective" don't admit their biases like we have, and constantly change the target while they argue for their own political and shifting outcomes of privatization of schooling while also moving away from early stated ends when they get "elusive" such as equity, student achievement, choice, etc.? (Lubienski, Brewer, & Malin, 2023)
- When we allow ourselves to become lackadaisical, unvigilant, and completely in some instances *unaware* that privateers are destroying the public good for private gain, breaking down communities, their history, their culture, their pride?

- When we give up on our responsibilities to maintain a public education system as a public good for all, even those who don't use it directly, that has largely been a beacon to the world, a lifeline for those seeking knowledge and advancement with little or no means, and a purveyor of opportunity, culture, beauty, and learning for centuries, despite the issues and problems that at times plague it?

Finally, when are we going to step up and defend public schooling, rebuild it, and fund it fairly and fully so that all can thrive? (Stitzlein, 2017)

So, Where Do We Go From Here?

The students in the class that produced this text have heard and participated in what I have said so far here, and much of it is reiterated from a significant, major influence: William L. Phillis and the Coalition for Equity and Adequacy of School Funding (Phillis, 2023). Bill is the founder and leader of this non-profit organization that has been fighting the good fight in Ohio since the Ohio Supreme Court found the over-reliance on property taxes to fund public schools to be in breach of the state's constitution decades ago, and while Ohio fought to reclaim its classrooms from the accountability thieves during the height of the testing and standardization movements, and now during the onslaught of privatization that he is fighting along with over 100 public school districts with a lawsuit called "Vouchers Hurt Ohio." What I want to say here about his work is how much I appreciate the relentless, smart, and even-handed rebuttal of the political stances that elected politicians and others are taking toward educational issues that hurt Ohioans. In the spirit of collegiality, academic freedom, and the dissemination of defensible and legitimate knowledge on the subject, we offer this text to examine the questions above, to surface more questions, to support the work of important advocates like William Phillis and organizations like Ohio E & A, and to take a stance on protecting and enhancing the value and reach of public education in our state and beyond.

To these ends, we offer five chapters in the body of this work in addition to this introduction, along with a short epilogue.

In Chapter 1: Democratic Accountability for Public Education, Abayomi Abodunrin, Mastano Dzimbiri, and Emmanuel Acheampong bring their unique, international educational perspectives to bear in framing the foundation of education as a critical aspect of western democracies, and how it can and should take shape as a public good.

In Chapter 2: How Charter Schools and Universal Vouchers Recolonize Communities, Tahreem Fatima, Hope Sweeney, and Chiquita Hughes lay the groundwork for understanding the importance of critical consciousness, and particularly the loss of it when schooling is privatized, as the voucher and charter movements re-colonize our schools, and further segregate the public.

In Chapter 3: Follow the Money, Tailyn Walborn, Carolyn Craig, and Dongxia Sang lay out how the money funding the voucher/charter movements, particularly in Ohio, works. Who wins? Who loses? And what are the deeper, further questions that we should be asking about how politics is playing such a major role in appropriating public money for private purposes?

In Chapter 4: Is School Choice Our Hope? An Imminent, Hidden Tragedy, Shawnieka E. Pope, Dormetria Robinson Thompson, and Jing Tan examine the tragic circumstances that follow the money, the human and societal losses that accrue when privateers sweep in to scenes of tragedy, and more often than not, wreak havoc and create even worse conditions for students.

In Chapter 5: The voucher movement is personal ~ Knowledge to action and manifesting (re)action, Cerelia V. Bizzell, Elizabeth Rae Kerr, and Jacqlyn Schott create a culminating, summary story for us to consider, in which they suggest ways forward—including an "Advocacy Action Items" checklist—for all to consider next steps for public action. We all need to be more involved in the politics surrounding school funding.

In the Epilogue, I provide an update on the situation in Ohio which took a significant turn with the signing of the new budget in July 2023 and its inclusion of significant new funding for vouchers.

A Final Introductory Note

It is also important to note that our approach to research for this project, using the currere method—with the ends in mind of having an impact through our advocacy scholarship on the discourse and action in education policy around the voucher and charter school movements—means that our text may include passages that we have created, including composite characters, even fictive passages. Pinar (1994) allows for the progressive phase of the currere approach to include our imaginations, dreams, insights, hopes. What might citizens think, hope for, and say when pressed to respond to the complex situations facing them with school choice? This doesn't make the passages any less real or factual, or scholarly.

Remember that the accurate, telling, moving, and historically accurate *The Things They Carried* (O'Brien, 2009) is a work of fiction, but no less important or effective in understanding the impact of the Vietnam War on American society and individuals than Karnow's *Vietnam: A History* (1983), in my opinion. This is a similar comparison to noting the relative strengths of say, Sizer's *Horace's Compromise* (1986) trilogy (Sizer used composite, fictional characters to frame his arguments) in relationship to Goodlad's *A Place Called School* (1984) study (Goodlad used longitudinal data culled by a large research team mainly to depict the nature and function of U.S. public schools at the time) and their overlapping understandings and hopes for America public schooling in the critical decade of the 1980s. What I am suggesting is that in this volume we are exploring many angles and possibilities for persuasion here, bringing multiple approaches, discourses, and stories to bear on the problem at hand. Let the reader decide if it is effective, helpful, meaningful, and how it fits in the landscape of other scholarship being produced on the topic at hand.

In addition, we didn't use Artificial Intelligence (AI) here in any way. It wasn't needed. We have our own intelligence and powers of discernment to draw on. You can be the judge about how effective our approach is or not in framing our advocacy for the public good through public schooling. In the end, though, our work is based on study, discussion, and imagination. After all, policy is borne out of imagination, and usually the policy wonks with the best story win out. Just ask those who have been forwarding the ideologically oriented, inaccurate policy documents and studies in support of vouchers and charters schools during the past decades. They typically reflect the ideological and political will of the authors and their funders. Will our advocacy scholarship here—in light of current and future policy around the voucher and charter school movements—be helpful, orienting, and perhaps transformative?

In the end, does our work move the needle? How does it hold up as scholarship? Does it make a difference?

—**Thomas S. Poetter**

References

Anderson, J. (1995). *The education of Blacks in the South, 1860–1935*. University of North Carolina Press.

Dyer, S., & Reedy, M. (2022, December). The promised education movement. *Columbus Bar Lawyer Quarterly, 7*(4), 30–36.

Garcia, D., & Steele, M. (2023). A voucher by any other name: Empowerment scholarship accounts and the future of school choice. In K. Welner, G.

Orfield, & L. Huerta (Eds.), *The school voucher illusion: Exposing the pretense of equity* (pp. 197–218). Teachers College Press.

Goodlad, J. (1984). *A place called school.* McGraw-Hill.

Gregory, T., & Smith, J. (1987). *High schools as communities: The small school reconsidered.* Phi Delta Kappa.

Gregory, T. (1993). *Making high school work.* Teachers College Press.

International Centre for Policy Advocacy. (2012). *Making research evidence matter: A guide to advocacy policy in transition countries* (https://advocacyguide.icpolicy advocacy.org/21-defining-policy-advocacy). Open Society Foundations.

Kaestle, C. (1983). *Pillars of the republic: Common schools and American society (1780–1860).* Hill and Wang.

Karnow, S. (1983). *Vietnam: A history.* Viking Press.

Lubienski, C., Brewer, T. J., & Malin, J. (2023). Bait and switch: How voucher advocates shift policy objectives. In K. Welner, G. Orfield, & L. Huerta (Eds.), *The school voucher illusion: Exposing the pretense of equity* (pp. 127–147). Teachers College Press.

Newmann, F., & Wehlage, G. (1995). *Successful school restructuring: A report to the public and educators by the Center on Organization and Restructuring of Schools.* National Association of Secondary School Principals.

O'Brien, T. (2009). *The things they carried.* Mariner Books.

Owen, H. (2008). *Open space techonology: A user's guide* (3rd ed.). Berrett-Koehler Publishers.

Phillis, W. (2023). The senate version of the state budget shows contempt for the people's governing document. Ohio Coalition for Equity and Adequacy of School Funding Blog: https://mail.google.com/mail/u/0/#search/Ohio+E+%26+A/WhctKKXxBvrtgSXWLFxTlNZnbRcNLSLCjgqdpxlwCwwbkLHSgdWLMPKgdmSvWnRpBvwHlgG

Pinar, W. (1994). The currere method. In *Autobiography, politics, and sexuality: Essays in curriculum theory 1972–1992* (Vol. 2, pp. 19–27). Peter Lang.

Pinar, W. (2012). *What is curriculum theory?* (2nd ed.). Routledge.

Poetter, T. (2003). James E. Loder: A life of love given freely to the hope and reality of transformation. *The Sophist's Bane, 1*(2), 9–12, 15.

Poetter, T. (1994). Making a difference: Miss Conner and Bunker Hill School. *Teaching Education Journal, 6*(1), 149–151.

Poetter, T., Pierson, J., Caivano, C., Stanley, S., Hughes, S., & Anderson, H. D. (1997). *Voices of inquiry in teacher education.* Lawrence Erlbaum Associates, Inc.

Poetter, T. (2010). Taking the leap, mentoring doctoral students as scholars: A great and fruitful morass. *Teaching & Learning: The Journal of Natural Inquiry & Reflective Practice, 24*(1), 22–29.

Poetter, T. S., & Googins, J. (Eds.). (2015). *Was someone mean to you today? The impact of standardization, corporatization, and high stakes testing on students, teachers, communities, schools, and democracy.* Van Griner Publishing.

Poetter, T. (2016). Opening curriculum windows: Curriculum pasts interpreted today by tomorrow's scholars. *Educational Practice & Reform Journal, 2*(1), 80–92.

Poetter, T. (2020). Curriculum theory and historical connections. In M. F. He & W. H. Schubert (Eds.), *Oxford encyclopedia of curriculum studies*. Oxford University Press. doi:10.1093/acrefore/9780190264093.013.1034

Sanders, R., Stoval, D., & White, T. (2018). *Twenty-first century Jim Crow schools: The impact of charters on public education*. Beacon Press.

Shimp, D., Vorys, W., & O'Donnell T. (2023, July). *Client alert: Ohio legislature passes biennial budget; Governor Dewine approaches historic investment in public education*. DickinsonWright.com.

Siddle Walker, V. (1996). *Their highest potential: An African American school community in the segregated South*. University of North Carolina Press.

Sizer, T. (1985). *Horace's compromise: The dilemma of the American high school*. Hougton Mifflin.

Sizer, T. (1997). *Horace's school: Redesigning the American high school*. Harper.

Stitzlein, S. (2017). *American public education and the responsibility of its citizens: Supporting democracy in the age of accountability*. Oxford Press.

Suitts, S. (2023). The segregationist origins and legacy of today's private school vouchers. In Welner, Orfield, & Huerta's (Eds.) *The school voucher illusion: Exposing the pretense of equity* (pp. 25–46). Teachers College Press.

Tyack, D. (1974). *The one best system: A history of American urban education*. Boston, MA: Harvard University Press.

Welner, K., Orfield, G., & Huerta, L. (2023). Voucher expansion and the abandonment of equity. In K. Welner, G. Orfield, & L. Huerta (Eds.), *The school voucher illusion: Exposing the pretense of equity* (pp. 1–24). Teachers College Press.

White, J., & Xu, C. (2022). *How are charter schools managed?* Retrieved from the National Alliance for Public Charter Schools website: https://data.publiccharters.org/digest/charter-school-data-digest/who-manages-charter-schools/

1

Democratic Accountability for Public Education

Abayomi Samuel Abodunrin
Mastano N. W. Dzimbiri
Emmanuel Acheampong

In recent decades, education systems worldwide have undergone profound transformations influenced by the ideologies of neoliberalism and the pursuit of educational choice. In the United States, these changes have sparked contentious debates about democratic accountability, particularly concerning the rise of charter schools and voucher programs. In this chapter, we explore and describe the intricate dynamics between democratic accountability in relation to the rapid growth of charter schools and voucher programs, and the pervasive influence of neoliberal principles in shaping the modern educational landscape.

At its core, the chapter aims to address a fundamental question: How do voucher programs and charter schools undermine the principles of democratic accountability, introducing injustices into an education system intended to be founded upon democratic ideals? Drawing from various theoretical frameworks, including Pinar's autobiographical method (1994) and the concepts of transparency and resistance put forth by Ben-Porath and Johanek (2019), we detail the undemocratic practices that emerged in the U.S. education system as a result of the ongoing expansion of voucher programs and charter schools. We have divided the chapter into the following sections. First, we provide a definition of democratic accountability and emphasize its significance in publicly funded schools. Our approach involves initiating a comprehensive dialogue about the effects of voucher and charter movements on the democratic accountability of publicly funded schools. Furthermore, we aim to examine the deep-rooted integration of neoliberal ideologies within the U.S. education system. This integration has gradually transformed the notion of education as a public "good" into a form of private property.

Alongside this analysis, we will explore alternative pathways to challenge the prevailing market-driven approach to education. Throughout the chapter, we assert that the progress driven by neoliberalism has substantially undermined the democratic principles that underpin the education system. As international graduate students in the Educational Leadership doctoral program on Leadership, Culture, and Curriculum, we bring our experiences to the table with the intention of fostering a deeper comprehension of the intricate dynamics involved in reconciling individual choice, market influences, and democratic accountability in the quest for inclusive and excellent education accessible to everyone.

Democratic Accountability and Its Significance in Education

Democratic accountability lies at the heart of any functioning democracy, ensuring that power remains vested in the hands of the people. Ben-Porath and Johanek (2019) define democratic accountability as "the ability of a community to control and demand a response from the institutions that serve it" (p. 11). They conceptualize democratic accountability into four aspects: transparency, participation, sanction, and resistance. In this chapter, however, we will focus on transparency and resistance as frameworks to better understand the state of democratic accountability in publicly funded schools in the United States given the rise of charter schools and the expansion of vouchers. Transparency as an aspect of democratic accountability highlights the role and nature of information available to support families' decision-making, and their ability to understand decision-making processes within instructions such as schools and districts (Ben-Porath & Johanek,

2019). Accountability through transparency "emphasizes the importance of accessible and reliable information" (Ben-Porath & Johanek, 2019, p. 15). Access to reliable information becomes crucial to effectively navigating the complexities of school choice.

For example, Abayomi shared, in our conversations as a writing team, his experience and the circumstances he encountered trying to enroll his son recently in kindergarten. He considered himself fortunate to have access to reliable information, which enabled him to make well-informed decisions. He dedicated significant time to extensive research and understood that not all parents were as privy to accessing such valuable information. As Hamilton and McEachin (2019) astutely highlight, families with lower incomes frequently encounter restricted resources and limited access to information, placing them at a disadvantage when searching for high-quality schools. Within an education system already burdened by financial disparities, the absence of reliable information further compounds the challenges faced by these families.

Resistance is also a critical component of understanding democratic accountability in education. Resistance plays a crucial role in comprehending governance within publicly funded institutions like schools, highlighting its significance in the context of democratic accountability. It involves seeking avenues to challenge policy decisions made based on public demand, as emphasized by Ben-Porath and Johanek (2019, pp. 105–106) in their examination of evidence-based resistance. Ben-Porath and Johanek argue that an essential aspect of the democratic process is to hold schools accountable by rejecting certain choices and demanding the expansion of existing limited options (p. 106). A notable example of resistance against the lack of democratic accountability was observed in the legal overturning of the Cleveland voucher program. The program, which allowed public funds to be used in private schools, faced criticism for violating the principle of separation between church and state. This concern was particularly significant as more than 80% of the participating private schools had religious affiliations (Fleeter, 2023). While the program faced subsequent repeals and legal battles, the U.S. Supreme Court ultimately upheld its legality in June 2002 (Fleeter, 2023).

The Scrunch for Financial Gain: Injustices, Accountability, and Money

As international graduate students from three African countries, we encountered significant difficulties when trying to understand the distinctions between public schools and charter schools in the U.S. education system. We were taken aback to learn that, unlike in countries such as Malawi, Ghana, and Nigeria, taxpayer funds in the United States are allocated to support charter schools. These schools are essentially privately owned institutions with a profit-driven focus, rather than prioritizing the social objectives and goals of education. As the conversation around charter schools intensifies and tension between private and public education in America emerges, concerns surface over time about how charter movements and voucher programs introduce injustice to the education system—one that is supposed to be built on the tenets of democratic accountability.

Over the years, schools have always been democratic spaces where accountability to both parents and students is seen as crucial to nurturing and educating students to become responsible democratic citizens. But at the moment, accountability, one of the distinguishing essences of schools, is being lost due to the defunding of public schools to support private education in the form of charters. Despite widespread skepticism and the fact that many charter schools are driven more by profit than by the needs of their students, the number of charter schools in the United States continues to grow rapidly. Legislators keep making consistent efforts to roll out voucher programs and other public streams of money that provide opportunities for people to access private and charter schools that have switched from the original motive for which they were established (Lubienski et al., 2009). Where lies the hope for public schools if funds intended for them are diverted to fund private schools and to enhance school choice through charter schools that often care less about being held accountable to parents and students?

Emmanuel, while sharing his story with our writing team, paints a picture of Kofi and Ama, two students of minority backgrounds who can only access public education by virtue of the fact that it is readily available to them, courtesy of state and government funding available for public education to ensure access to students who cannot afford the luxury of private education. Kofi and Ama, children of Ghanaian parents who are struggling to make ends meet in America, will have no choice but to enroll their wards in public schools with the hope that the education system will meet the needs of their children, who will become generational leaders and could ameliorate the financial condition of the family in the future. This means that, aside from the schools serving as spaces for students to gain relevant knowledge to become significant future citizens, they also serve as a place of hope for parents who believe their children will help them out of their current situation of hardship in the near future.

Schools, therefore, in our democratic world today, have the responsibility to be accountable to such parents and other educational stakeholders, as such accountability strengthens the trust parents have in the education system and makes them hopeful for a brighter future. Accountability has always been the hallmark of public education, as teachers are supposed to disclose students' performance to parents, and parents are also given the opportunity to participate in and contribute to the educational progress of their wards. With the rise of charter schools, accountability is being lost. Charter schools act autonomously and may be less attentive to the demands and interests of parents and students. It just places too much emphasis on test results. In our democratic world today, judging the quality of education should not just center on test scores but also on the commitment of schools to providing education tailored to meet the interests and needs of parents and students. This goes a long way toward determining the choice of schools that parents select for their children. Parents are interested in schools that can meet the needs of their children, are accountable, and bring out the best in them. Elizabeth Kerr, one of our doctoral colleagues who doubles as a mother said that, in relocating to Cincinnati, one of her worries was searching for a school that would meet the needs of her kids. She said,

> This district, we found, had open enrollment, but it was convoluted and unclear how to apply. There were a few charter schools in our area, all of which touted results that surpassed those of the public schools. And, finally, we qualified for the coveted voucher. Yet, we'd still end up paying out of pocket, and none of the private schools in the area seemed very impressive. School choice was abundant, but my decision as a parent was, and is, difficult. What option would provide the most opportunity for my child? Which schools would work best with our schedules? In which schools would my child feel welcome and like she belonged?

From her fragments, it is quite evident that choice isn't the problem here, but what schools have to offer her children. This is what is so dear to her heart. Accountable schools place emphasis on openness, information, and collaboration to establish an educational environment that makes it possible for students to thrive. Democracies rest on the combination of two ideas: that those who rule should do so in the public interest or in response to the public will, and that they will be more likely to do so when they are in some way representative of and/or accountable to those they rule. This assertion is a corollary of the importance of accountability in raising democratic citizens. Educational institutions are supposed to be democratic institutions that utilize the concept of accountability to meet the interests of their stakeholders. But there is a high level of injustice associated with charter schools: from the discrimination meted out to minorities who attempt to attend charter schools, such as students being denied enrollment into charter schools because of their disability and students with special needs being ignored, punished, and even bullied in charter schools; to charter schools forcing students to pay fines of approximately $200,000 per year for minor infractions while also causing students to repeat entire years for failing a single class to the firing of school employees, without any reasonable justification; to the use of funds meant for public schools funding voucher programs for already affluent students to get access to private education at the expense of the "have nots" without any reasonable accountability system (Sanders et al., 2018). It is clear that accountability is losing its place in our educational space, especially now that more efforts are geared towards funding Education Savings Accounts (ESAs) and other voucher programs.

Among the numerous challenges faced by charter schools is the issue of accountability. It has always been difficult to ascertain the welfare of charter schools because of the lack of data about them. Among the reasons for the establishment of charter schools was that they would be more accountable than traditional schools because they would have to meet the demands of parents and students. But now we have charters that care less about what becomes of students and parents, as their interest is often merely based on the financial gains available to them. The accountability process has a positive democratic effect when it contributes to improved communication and epistemic quality, supports democratic standards and criteria of the assessment, contributes to political equality, and helps citizens find meaning in life through reflection and reasoning together, possibly internalizing a democratic civic ethos.

Implications of Vouchers and Charter Schools on Democratic Accountability

Our discussion in this section rests on ways in which the expansion of voucher programs and charter school movements contributes to the erosion of democratic accountability in the U.S. public education system and, of course, beyond. In the realm of education, democratic accountability traditionally involves robust public oversight and control over schools, with elected officials and school boards responsible for decision-making processes. However, the rise of neoliberalism, an ideology that promotes free markets and individual choice, has challenged this conventional understanding of democratic accountability in education. One manifestation of this shift is the growth of charter schools. Charter schools are publicly funded but operate independently, and often exempt from certain regulations that govern traditional public schools.

The voucher and charter movements have introduced significant changes to the education landscape, offering alternative options to traditional public schools. However, these movements have also sparked debates regarding their impact on democratic accountability within the education system. On the negative side, there is growing evidence that voucher and charter schools have reduced public oversight compared to traditional public schools. Thus, voucher programs often allow private entities to manage educational institutions, diminishing the influence of the broader community. This shift in decision-making authority to private entities or unelected boards erodes democratic accountability as key governance and policy decisions are made without direct public input. Moreover, the expansion of voucher programs and charter schools has led to a reduction in funding for public schools, resulting in a notable deterioration in the quality of public education.

According to Black (2013), this has also exacerbated the growing disparity in access to education based on socioeconomic status and racial background. Besides, the democratic ideal of collective decision-making and shared responsibility is undermined when important educational choices are entrusted to entities with limited public accountability. Critics argue that voucher and charter schools exacerbate educational inequalities and promote segregation within the education system. By enabling selectivity in student admissions based on various factors, such as academic performance or geographic location, these movements create a stratified system. Privileged students may have access to schools that offer better resources and opportunities, while less advantaged students are left with fewer resources and support. This perpetuates disparities in educational outcomes and undermines the democratic principle of equal access to quality education for all.

As scholars of educational policy, we share the concerns raised by critics regarding the diminishing democratic accountability within public education, primarily attributed to voucher programs and charter schools. One of the key issues lies in the fact that the governing boards of these schools are frequently not elected democratically, leading to potential challenges in transparency and public oversight. This lack of democratic process raises valid concerns and aligns us with the critics' viewpoint. Nevertheless, voucher programs are there to divert revenues from public schools to private schools, and these schools do not report to the government on how the funds are used. These educational reforms, rooted in neoliberal ideologies, have prompted intense debate while raising fundamental questions about the role of the state in promotion if them.

Neoliberal policies have not only wreaked havoc on the education system in the United States but have also eroded transparency and social justice by impeding equitable access to public education in developing countries. These detrimental outcomes can be attributed to the implementation of structural adjustment programs promoted by Western institutions, namely the World Bank and the IMF. In the context of structural adjustment programs, several African countries, like Malawi, adopted policies that introduced tuition fees in public schools, primarily targeting secondary schools and universities. The government's focus on privatizing state-owned institutions has led to reduced funding for these schools, posing notable financial hardships for parents from low-income households.

Consequently, parents encounter difficulties in meeting the costs of tuition fees and other education-related expenses required for their children. Given the racial segregation in the United States, the ongoing proliferation of charter schools and the expansion of voucher programs raise significant concerns regarding the diversion of public resources from traditional public schools to these so-called "charter schools" that often operate more like private institutions (Bartlett et al., 2002; Rubin et al., 2021). This situation prompts essential questions about the justification behind redirecting public funds to institutions that, despite claiming to be public, often function as private entities.

Considering the operational characteristics of charter schools, we contend that their existence has resulted in not only the erosion of accountability, a fundamental principle in democratic societies, but also the exacerbation of inequalities in access to education. Thus, it is crucial to recognize that low-income communities and people of color are disproportionately affected by the consequences of school choice programs, such that children from elite families are more likely to benefit from vouchers compared to those from low socio-economic backgrounds (Malin et al., 2019). Stahl's (2017) ethnographic study *Neoliberal School: Building Cultures of Success* exposes how neoliberal policies, driven by market forces, competition, and an emphasis on high-stakes standardized testing within meritocratic policies, create hindrances for students from under-resourced or economically disadvantaged school districts, preventing them from accessing higher education.

The goal of neoliberal policies is not simply to provide families with options for selecting schools of their choice for children, but rather, their ultimate intention is to systematically exclude a specific group of individuals from accessing the benefits of public education and hindering their ability to become well-informed citizens. The prevailing discourse has primarily revolved around whether charters and vouchers can yield improved educational outcomes, often defined narrowly as enhanced test scores (Black, 2013). However, setting aside the contentious debate over whether charters or vouchers genuinely enhance student achievement, it is essential to recognize that the notion of "better" among charter school advocates, typically refers to the outcomes experienced by students who participate in these options, rather than considering the overall impact on the education system as a whole (Black, 2013). Black further contends that failure to address these fundamental issues neglects the broader concerns regarding what constitutes public good in education. Therefore, our argument is that neoliberal policies in education act more like weapons of mass destruction as they perpetuate systemic and structural massacres of public education, fostering knowledge apartheid as citizens are denied their rights and freedom to access quality public education.

Urban–Rural Dichotomy: A Story from Abayomi

During my visits to a rural school district near Toledo, Ohio, I was continuously surprised at the impact of relatively higher funding levels in rural settlements. These schools had access to better resources, modern facilities, and advanced technology, all of which contributed to creating a conducive learning environment. The commitment to education was evident in the well-equipped classrooms, up-to-date textbooks, and ample extracurricular opportunities provided to students. I experienced middle school students engaging in robotic engineering. This came as a surprise and a shock to me to witness such a high level of education at that level. In this regard, I was intrigued when informed that I would also be visiting some public schools in urban areas in that region. My experience in these urban schools shed light on the challenges they faced. Insufficient funding led to overcrowded classrooms, outdated materials, and a lack of essential resources and an overall lack of opportunity for many students.

Teachers in urban schools often had to grapple with limited support and inadequate infrastructure, making it challenging to deliver quality education to their students. The contrast between schools in urban areas and those in more affluent rural communities was disheartening. In these urban areas, inadequate resources and outdated facilities plagued the schools, hindering the learning process. Overcrowded classrooms, limited technology, and worn-out textbooks painted a grim picture of the obstacles faced by both teachers and students. Similarly, my first introduction to school choice in the United States occurred during this period when I visited a charter school in Toledo, Ohio. I remember asking one of our American coordinators what charter school meant. Even though she tried her best to explain things to me, I just could not comprehend. You cannot blame me because I had never heard of such a term until that moment. Nevertheless,

I was expecting a great experience, unfortunately, my anticipation for an improved learning environment quickly transformed into astonishment as I stepped into the elementary school. The entire student population, spanning various age groups, was crammed into a single classroom. The lack of age-appropriate divisions, educational resources, and specialized instruction was deeply troubling.

Shifting Focus: Challenging the Market-Driven Approach

Over the years, pro-public education groups have consistently drawn attention to the long-standing market-driven approach to public education. As we worked on this chapter, Abayomi shared a personal experience involving families whose children attend urban public schools in some parts of the United States. For these families, school choice represented a glimmer of hope, providing them with a sense of optimism for the future. The allure of opting for an alternative educational option through policy reforms held great appeal to these families.

They saw it as a potential pathway to secure a brighter future for their children, one that encompassed well-funded schools equipped with modern facilities and high-quality instruction.

However, the families soon came to realize that the journey toward attaining school choice was fraught with numerous challenges. The ongoing expansion of charter schools and voucher programs in distressed urban districts has sparked considerable debate and contention. It is evident that these expansions are significantly transforming the governance, structure, and purpose of public education, particularly in high-poverty urban areas. Given the numerous challenges faced by urban schools in delivering quality education, it comes as no surprise that proponents of school choice policy are leveraging this opportunity to promote their agendas, platforms, and vested financial interests.

Besides, drawing upon our experiences, we have managed to draw parallels between the educational disparities within the U.S. educational system, which is assumed to be built upon democratic principles. Through this, we have recognized the existing disparities and understand how they affect students' educational achievements. Our experiences studying in the United States have made us realize that these educational inequalities based on geography are manifestations of charter schools/voucher programs under the school choice policy (Lubienski et al., 2009).

Contrary to our initial thoughts, we were surprised to learn that the quality of education in rural areas frequently exceeded that of urban schools.

Nevertheless, we acknowledge that this discrepancy is rooted in the pronounced disparities in school funding, which heavily favor more affluent residents residing in rural areas. This advantage is primarily attributed to the reliance on property taxes as a funding mechanism, which perpetuates inequalities in educational resources and opportunities. In order to challenge this prevailing trend, we agree with the ideas of Horsford et al. (2018) regarding a "resistance philosophy." This entails forming a counter coalition that actively pushes for policies aimed at reinvesting in public schools, irrespective of geography (Horsford et al., 2018), while taking equity into consideration. Therefore, by embracing this approach, we can work towards reversing the negative impact of market-driven reforms and prioritizing the well-being and improvement of the public education system.

Undemocratic Nature of the Movements

By "undemocratic nature of the movements" we refer to the characteristics or aspects of voucher movements and charter schools in the context of policies, or actions that contradict or undermine democratic principles and values within the education system. As described earlier in this chapter, in a democratic society, power is vested in the hands of the people, and decisions are made through processes that ensure representation, participation, and transparency. Our critical analysis of this educational policy issue in regard to what is currently at stake in the U.S. education system reveals that the voucher movement and charter schools encounter serious transparency challenges such that, allocation of funds through these programs/movements lacks accountability, limited information, huge risks of unequal access to quality education, potential fraud, as well as abuse of public resources. These malpractices exemplify undemocratic societies that deliberately withhold transparency on public expenditures from the general population. In such environments, information about how the allocation and utilization of public funds is intentionally concealed, limiting the public's ability to hold authorities accountable for their actions.

On the other hand, resistance to vouchers emerges from worries about their impact on public institutions, doubts regarding the quality of private providers, concerns about equity erosion, political opposition, and the absence of standardized educational standards. Striking a balance between promoting choice and addressing these concerns is crucial for ensuring equitable access to quality education, while also maintaining accountability and safeguarding public services. Policymakers must carefully consider these issues to create effective voucher programs that benefit the broader population.

Additionally, public participation is an integral component of democratic accountability. Engaging parents, educators, and community members in discussions and decision-making about voucher programs and charter schools can lead to more inclusive and responsive policies. Actively involving stakeholders can help policymakers gain valuable insights and perspectives that inform the design and implementation of these programs. Policymakers can foster a more equitable and accountable education system that benefits all students and upholds democratic principles and values by addressing the challenges associated with transparency while also promoting active participation.

Conclusion and Summary

Charter schools receive public funding but are usually exempt from some state regulations due to their charter agreements (Ben-Porath & Johanek, 2019). This exemption limits their ability to develop the public and civic aspects traditionally integral to public schools. We can see that the erosion of the public and common good raises significant alarms, as it compromises the fundamental principles that public schools have long stood for. Market-driven charter schools emphasize individual achievement rather than collective well-being. However, for families to make informed decisions, they need access to useful information. Unfortunately, we have observed that the policies and programs associated with these schools lack mechanisms to facilitate information gathering and sharing.

Additionally, charter schools receiving public funds often operate with minimal government regulation, and are not built to foster parental participation (Berliner, 2022). In this regard, participating schools are not obligated to provide access to crucial school records, budgets, or administration details. The absence of external authority to assess curriculum, attendance, disciplinary measures, special education policies, and practices further exacerbates the accountability gap (Finn et al., 2009). It becomes evident that public funds are being allocated to schools through voucher programs without adequate attention to accountability measures.

We firmly believe that choosing the right school for our children requires careful consideration of their unique needs, interests, and learning styles. It is essential to find an educational environment that fosters their growth and provides opportunities for them to thrive. However, in an increasingly unregulated market where state subsidies play a significant role, making well-informed choices becomes a challenging task. Furthermore, it is the undeniable responsibility of the government to ensure equitable access to education for all citizens, yet these policies brazenly undermine this crucial obligation. We are convinced that the autonomy in the operation of charter schools in contrast to traditional public schools gives rise to concerns regarding accountability and transparency in the utilization of public resources. We strongly believe that the privatization of public education through vouchers and charter schools has resulted in an erosion of democratic accountability as the owners prioritize market-oriented principles, reduce government oversight, and narrow the focus on educational goals and outcomes.

References

Bartlett, L., Frederick, M., Gulbrandsen, T., & Murillo, E. (2002). The marketization of education: Public schools for private ends. *Anthropology & Education Quarterly, 33*(1), 5–29.

Black, D. W. (2013). Charter schools, vouchers, and the public good. *Wake Forest Law Review, 48*, 445–488. https://scholarcommons.sc.edu/cgi/viewcontent.cgi?article=1960&context=law_facpub

Blakely, J. (April 17, 2017). How school choice turns education into a commodity: Schools as a public good under threat. *The Atlantic.* https://www.theatlantic.com/education/archive/2017/04/is-school-choice-really-a-form-of-freedom/523089/

Diem, S., & Brooks, J. S. (2022). Critical policy analysis in education: Exploring and interrogating (in)equity across contexts: Special issue introduction. *Education Policy Analysis Archives, 30*(10). https://doi.org/10.14507/epaa.30.7340

Horsford, S. D., Scott, J. T., & Anderson, G. L. (2018). *The politics of education policy in an era of inequality: Possibilities for democratic schooling.* Routledge.

Lubienski, C., Gulosino, C., & Weitzel, P. (2009). School choice and competitive incentives: Mapping the distribution of educational opportunities across local education markets. *American Journal of Education, 115*, 601–647.

Malin, J. R., Lubienski, C., & Mensa-Bonsu, Q. (2020). Media strategies in policy advocacy: Tracing the justifications for Indiana's school choice reforms. *Educational Policy, 34*(1), 118–143.

Malin, J. R., Hardy, I., & Lubienski, C. (2019). Educational neoliberalization: The mediatization of ethical assertions in the voucher debate. *Discourse: Studies in the Cultural Politics of Education, 40*(2), 217–233.

Pinar, W. F. (1994). *Autobiography, politics, and sexuality: Essays in curriculum theory 1972–1992.* Peter. Lang Publishing.

Rubin, J. S., & Weber, M. (2021). Charter schools' impact on public education: Theory versus reality. In C. H. Tienken & C. A. Mullen (Eds.), *The risky business of education policy* (pp. 72–87). Routledge.

Stahl, G. (2017). *Ethnography of a neoliberal school: Building cultures of success* (Vol. 14). Routledge.

2

How Charter Schools and Universal Vouchers Recolonize Communities

Tahreem Fatima
Hope Porta Sweeney
Chiquita M. Hughes

Norman Rockwell placed an indelible image on the psyche of Americans in his painting *The Problem We All Live With* (https://en.wikipedia.org/wiki/The_Problem_We_All_Live_With). The painting depicts deep-seated racism and resistance to desegregation that required U.S. Marshals to escort Ruby Bridges (and her mother) as she integrated for the first time William Frantz Elementary, an all-White school in New Orleans. At the tender age of six years, Ruby learned that the color of her skin mattered and was the cause of vehement and angry faces that communicated, "We don't want you here!"

More than 60 years have passed since the nation watched the horrific verbal assaults directed at little Ruby Bridges. Yet, the messaging of segregation persists in the voucher movement that clearly communicates to one group of students, "We don't want you here!" This messaging is heard and felt by students and their families. The hideousness of segregation's impact on society has not only been experienced in the South, but also across the United States. Justice Earl Warren in *Brown v Board of Education* (1954) captured the essence of segregation and its impact on Black children in stating that segregation, "generates a feeling of inferiority as to their status in the community" (Ben-Porath & Johanek, 2019, p. 59).

There were so many issues that surfaced as we considered our positionalities and personal contexts in applying currere to this chapter. Each of our perspectives evolved from a critical analysis of the problem of vouchers and charter schools as vehicles to recolonize public schools and communities. We collectively view education as a public good that is inclusive, uniting, and empowering for both students and communities. We agree that communities and families should have the ability to determine the location, methods, and curriculum of their student's education. We agree that charter schools and private schools that accept vouchers operate in a manner that is colonizing, or recolonizing, and that this tactic has a little-known negative history in the United States that dates back to the *Brown* decision in 1954 in which desegregation of all public schools became a requirement. We agree that, specifically, a lack of critical consciousness and desire for economic and political power and control directly contribute to the support of charter schools and most recently, the push for universal vouchers.

In this chapter, we explain how a sustained lack of critical consciousness has led some to a misguided belief in these segregating education options that seek to recolonize communities and create a caste system of the haves and have nots. We will discuss how that same lack of critical consciousness is maintained within the privatized walls of charter schools and funded by voucher programs. To help our readers understand the colonizing effects, we will provide descriptions that give historical and current context of concepts and processes that are at play. We will work to provide definitions to the terms we use including terms commonly used by proponents of charters and voucher systems. Primarily, we aim to deepen our understanding of the issues that vouchers, charter, and private schools present. Second, we aim to center the many lives that have been and still are adversely affected by vouchers and the privatization of education. Last, we aim to use this reflective process to imagine possibilities that would return the view of public education as a public good for all children.

The Problems Defined

A charter school is a public school created through a charter with the state, a school district, or some other public entity. State charter school statutes typically relieve charter schools of state and local regulations and, in return, charter schools agree that renewal of their charters will be contingent on their success in improving student academic achievement. President Bill Clinton called charters the "schools without rules" (Heubert, 1997). The goal of the original charter school proponents was to allow charters to provide room for innovation and an alternative to a public school system that they claimed was broken. Proponents promised increases in test scores and overall outcomes when compared to traditional public schools.

But charter schools and, later, voucher programs, have yet to fulfill the promises of providing a high-quality education for students whose needs weren't supposedly being met in the public schools (Sanders et al., 2018). Charter schools have not delivered the promises they've made and, in fact, some charter schools have engaged in deceitful practices in order to assert political and ideological control over the face of the future, i.e., our children. Charter school students nationwide have lower NAEP reading and math scores than traditional public school (TPS) students in both 4th and 8th grades, and lower science scores in 8th grades (Epple et al., 2016, p. 10). Dyer and Reedy (2022) noted that "the average Ohio charter school has a lower four-year graduation rate than all but one public school district" (p. 30), and that "Ohio's charters have received more F grades than A, B and C *combined*" (p. 31). The Ohio education choice program is, as admitted by David Brennan, a founding father of Ohio's EdChoice Scholarship program, a political movement, not an educational one, and it has "exacerbated the racial resegregation of our schools and communities" (p. 31). How have we come to a point in which the state is considering the expansion of a failing, historically segregating replacement educational model rather than repairing the public system that was built and continues to have the potential to meet the needs of students of all levels within their own cultures and communities?

School vouchers provide education tax dollars that are diverted from public schools to help subsidize the tuition of private and religious schools (nsba.org, 2023). In fact, our readings focused on this type of school choice originating in southern communities opposed to desegregation (Ben-Porath & Johanek, 2017; Hosford et al., 2019). School choice through vouchers is not a new phenomenon. The evolution of vouchers has been fueled by the fact that there is general consensus on a few propositions. Vouchers are exclusive. Vouchers are rooted in a type of separatism that is shrouded in parental rights and parental choice. During the evolution of vouchers from the 1950s to now, there are seminal characteristics that are undeniable. Historically, vouchers have favored those who are economically privileged in the middle to upper social classes, politically conservative, residents of suburban neighborhoods, and mostly White families. Despite the "new opportunities" touted by proponents, 70–80% of vouchers in Arizona, Missouri, and Wisconsin are given to students already in private schools (Cowen, 2023).

We Have to Understand the History

As we noted earlier, vouchers came first as a tactic in the American South to bypass desegregation laws after the *Brown* decision. They were created by southern segregationists (Suitts, 2023, p. 25) who were at first bold in their racist, nationalist pontifications (p. 27), but over time honed their ability to veil racism in more politically correct wording (p. 29). The result was a series of laws and constitutional amendments across seven southern states that provided protection and financial support to "largely unregulated private schools" that were attended by White students escaping public school desegregation (p. 25). Today, 27 states, including 11 Southern states, have developed similar school choice programs. The segregationist calls for "freedom of choice" in the South echo in today's calls for national programs of "school choice." By 1965, most of the voucher programs were determined to be unconstitutional (p. 38) and discriminatory. It is the "unexamined legacy" of segregationists' strategies to avoid desegregation that has expanded from racist tendencies to the exclusion of students with disabilities and, as in the case of Indiana and Florida, students in the LGBTQIA+ community (Cowen, 2023).

Ohio was the second state after Wisconsin to enact vouchers in 1996 (Abrams & Koutsavlis, 2023, p. 14) and has expanded to now include six separate voucher programs. In 2008, Ohio's spending on voucher programs was $69,772,755 and had increased to a total of $360,646,965 in 2019 (p. 14). Next school year, 2023–2024, spending will approach or exceed $1 Billion. Charter schools reported spending $13,426 per pupil while in the same time period public school funding per pupil increased from $11,148 to $12,736. However, when broken down, charter schools spent $3,000 of that total on administrative costs as opposed to public school administrative spending that averaged $1,856 (Dyer & Reedy, 2022; Epple et al., 2016). Because of the number of vouchers and the spending that has occurred, Ohio is called the

"Wild, Wild west of Charter Schools" (p. 31). As more funding goes to charters and vouchers, essentially private entities, communities are further damaged as there are fewer dollars for needs such as public transit, parks, libraries, and public schools (Abrams & Koutsavlis, 2023, p. 16). To make matters worse, 1 in 4 charter schools close within the first five years (Dyer & Reedy, 2022; Cowen, 2023). This instability results in poor outcomes for students and the upheaval leaves scars on the community as promises are unfulfilled, public school programs are displaced, and money is lost.

Smith (2001), writing about the development in the late 1800s–1900s of private residential indigenous schools in the United States and Canada, noted that education is never politically neutral in a colonial context, that it always bears a notable burden of the colonializing process (p. 267), and 22 years later, Lubienski et al. (2023) write, "...we conclude that advocacy around vouchers is much more a manifestation of a political/ideological agenda than of an empirically based effort to remedy educational inequity noting how efforts by advocates to shift their own criteria for evaluating their preferred policy proposals represents a significant concern for the scholarly community, policymakers, and stakeholders" (p. 128). What is that ideology? It is one of the oldest in our nation, the colonizer's desire for expansion of power and reach for wealth. How can I (Hope) draw such a conclusion? Because I lived the colonizer's experience.

*　*　*

The small white milk cartons with green writing and pictures of Africa on them were each marked with the name of a student in my class. We had all shaken them to let the others hear the loose change rattle inside before placing them on the teacher's desk. Now sitting, facing forward, uniforms neat and ready for the day, we waited to hear which of us had collected enough spare change from our homes to edge out the rest of the class as the top contributor to the charity collection. It was a competition, not an exercise in empathy or an attempt to encourage critical consciousness. We had not learned about the people in African countries, we had not seen pictures of the existing homes or cities or culture. We had been shown dehumanizing, still pictures of emaciated children and told that they required our saving. We heard words like war and famine, but in that small, private school classroom in 1980, we had no real idea of what that meant. Our daily, well-orchestrated lives gave us no frame of reference. There was no lesson to help the students embrace the idea of equality and human rights. And so, we also did not understand the implication of a missionary going into another country to establish a physical mission, to teach the people

English, capitalism, and religion. I knew I was not the top collector, but I had contributed some, and while I didn't have words for it at that age, it gave me the feeling of being complicit rather than compassionate.

Providing the Model

Private and parochial schools were an early model of charter schools, more than 100 years before the latter was conceived. The U.S. government's post-Civil War "policy of aggressive civilization" allowed for schools built and funded by the government and run by religious organizations, and intended to civilize and assimilate indigenous populations (Smith, 2001; Hagan, 1988). Private and parochial schools have a history of locating in minoritized areas and subjugating communities, indoctrinating students, requiring assimilation to a specific cultural norm, sometimes forcibly requiring attendance of the private school (Smith, 2001; Hagan, 1988; Davis, 2004), and lobbying for public funding of a religious (private) affiliated organization. They have indeed presented a theoretical blueprint for the structure of charter schooling and now have an easy time of melding into the charter school landscape. They have found a way to remedy the declining attendance and rising tuition costs of private/parochial schools (a reduction in economics and power) by thinly veiling a political agenda and taking full advantage of the charter school push.

A Colonizer, Colonized

The sun hadn't fully risen when I (Hope), a second grader, got on the bus carrying my lunch and wearing the school uniform my mom had gotten from the swap after church. I was careful not to scuff the new shoes my mother had splurged on. I didn't recognize any of the riders on this bus. They weren't the students I'd gone to school with for the past two years. No, they were much older than me and none of them wore a uniform. These students were headed to the local public middle and high schools.

The driver directed me to the seat directly behind him. I sat quietly and watched the pastures and hay fields pass by my window as we drove the two or three miles to the elementary school I'd been attending. The school, which held grades K–5, was not scheduled to open for a few more hours, so when we arrived, I got off the bus, and stood on the sidewalk outside the mostly dark school and waited for the next bus that would arrive to take me to the private school another 15 or so minutes away, on the other side of our small town.

As the minutes passed, a few more buses arrived and dropped off more uniform-clad students. I didn't know them or where they had come from, but they were dressed in the same uniform and waiting on the same bus. This was so different from my morning routine in previous school years and I wasn't sure why the change had happened. I liked my school and the teachers and friends I had there. I didn't understand that the private school across town taught grades two through eight or that the church my family belonged to required me to attend the attached parochial school when I reached the second grade. I did not know that word of mouth was that the local public schools should be avoided or that the parochial school billed itself as more advanced than the public schools. I did not know yet that some of my new teachers were the religious sisters I had seen sitting together in a segregated group in church.

My mother had made the same choice for my four older siblings before me, paying the tuition for each in the form of required tithing each Sunday. The parochial school had economically and religiously recolonized my community. The school had placed its values upon me, my family, and the families of each student. The parochial school required attendance, and then charged each family for the promise of better education among people of better character. And over time that pervasive mindset was conveyed to me and my classmates in a hundred little ways through lessons and glances and offhand remarks. Not a shot had been fired, but the war was well underway.

* * *

Colonization is several actions in one process. It is settling among and establishing control over (subjugating) the indigenous people of an area (Oxford Dictionary, n.d.), exploiting them and appropriating that place as a domain for one's own use as an extension of state power (Merriam-Webster Dictionary, n.d.), often while forcing the colonizer's own language and cultural values upon the subjugated people (Blakemore, 2021). This is the process by which the United States was created and expanded, and it is used by many private and charter schools to recolonize economically and racially minoritized communities, thereby widening the gaps between the haves and the have nots. Colonization is and has been reified through economic, social, and cultural domination. Power, property, and economics are at the center of colonization. Neocolonialism, like neoliberalism, uses capitalism, globalization, and cultural forces to control in lieu of direct military or political control. While touting choice and the free market, these concepts also lead to manipulation and control (Apple, 2006; Giroux 2005). The expansion and proliferation of voucher programs and charter schools have led to processes that mirror these colonial dynamics in several ways.

1. *Power:* Charter schools, much like colonizers, exert power and control over marginalized communities. The establishment of charter schools in economically disadvantaged areas does not adequately involve or empower local communities in decision-making processes. Charter schools have their own governance structures, do not have locally elected boards, and in some cases are run by large corporations who operate schools in multiple states. Parents have little say in the daily operations or educational tactics of the school. While the original assumption regarding charter school placement was that they would locate in more affluent communities, the opposite has actually occurred. Charter schools tend to locate in urban areas with high concentrations of minority and low-income students. This is the primary factor giving rise to the high degree of segregation by race/ethnicity and by FRL [free and reduced lunch] status that characterizes the majority of charter schools (Epple et al., 2015, p. 16).
2. *Displacement:* Charter schools, supported by outside organizations and corporations, can displace traditional public schools and disrupt local educational systems. This displacement can be seen as analogous to colonization's impact on indigenous cultures and communities, where existing cultural and economic structures are determined inferior to and therefore supplanted by the external influences. Aside from racial divisions, students with disabilities are not typically served by charter schools lending to additional segregation and marginalization of those students. Education becomes market driven and the students become the commodity rather than the consumer.
3. *Cultural Assimilation:* Charter schools, often driven by standardized testing and rigid curriculum requirements, can perpetuate a one-size-fits-all educational model that prioritizes assimilation into dominant cultural norms. This can disregard the diverse cultural identities and needs of marginalized communities, mirroring aspects of colonization that sought to erase already existing cultures.
4. *Privatization and Inequality:* The growth of charter schools and voucher programs can lead to the privatization of education and exacerbate existing educational inequities. The diversion of public funds away from traditional public schools (TPS) may result in reduced resources and opportunities for traditional public schools, leading to increased disparities in educational access and outcomes. Currently, charter schools lobby state and city governments for additional monies stating that they do not have the funds to educate the students they serve. Private schools are experiencing

reduced enrollment, and in many cases have had to consolidate or close all together. How then does further dividing out students and funding help to improve educational quality? In an effort to exert power, ideas such as the Cincinnati Classical Academy (CCA) charter school are coming onto the educational scene. According to their website, The CCA was "founded by a group of local citizens who care deeply about our civic society and national heritage." It is located in a former catholic school building in Reading (available because the school was forced to close due to decreasing attendance), still owned by the Cincinnati Archdiocese and leased to CCA. It is under the sponsorship of St. Aloysius Catholic School which runs multiple charter schools in Ohio including a similar academy in Toledo (Hillsdale.edu). The CCA website also notes that it prioritizes admission of Reading public school district students and that the goal of the liberal arts curriculum at CCA, created by conservative Hillsdale College, aims "to instill appreciation of the Good, the True, and the Beautiful, as revealed through the Western and Judeo-Christian traditions." A cursory look at the Hillsdale College website shows a statement soliciting donations to help them in maintaining independence by not accepting any governmental monies, lectures on the decline of American citizenship, and a weekly sponsored podcast that often discusses the perceived failings of liberal politics.

These processes make vouchers a tool of colonization. In tandem, power and displacement are used to promote cultural assimilation. Vouchers and neoliberalism operate in a reciprocal relationship. Neoliberalism in education, a/k/a market-driven approaches, utilizes vouchers and privatization for legalized inequality. Consequently, the disparities are conspicuous as public schools (mostly urban) have considerably fewer resources to provide a quality education for students. Some scholars, like Giroux (2005), consider market-based policies as an evil attack on traditional public schools, which serve as a vehicle for social and economic reproduction (Apple, 2006; Giroux, 2005). In other words, generations of "the haves" continue and so do the generations of the "have nots." Now, whose children deserve to be forced to endure mandatory laws designed to ensure that their lives would never reach a status of equality to the lives of children in the dominant culture? Through legal jurisprudence and dismissive politics, Black and Brown children are not expected to reach the level of aspirational capital that they or their parents hold for them. The objective of charter schooling and universal vouchers is not equality but inequality veiled as choice (Giroux, 2005).

Private is not the Panacea

I (Hope) never imagined that I would be an educator. To be completely honest, I'd spent most of my life vowing never to be like the educators in my pre-baccalaureate years. But who I am as an educator today has everything to do with my past educational experiences. This project has been eye-opening, validating, and frustrating for me as I utilized the currere method to process my experience of schooling and held it up against the backdrop of educational history.

While reading Golann's (2021) *Scripting the Moves* as a part of the pre reading preparation for this writing project, I was unphased by the descriptions of the well-outlined behavioral expectations of students and teachers in the Knowledge is Power Program (KIPP) charter schools. KIPP is a corporation of charter schools serving 20 states and over 100,000 students (p. 1). Their no excuses ethos has made KIPP a model for others but I find it strange that they specifically focus on scripting behavior, and are focused on social control rather than curriculum and pedagogy. Yes, order matters, but I can relate to a student feeling constantly controlled, pinned down, and having no autonomy at all. That is the opposite of democratic education and I contend that it does not prepare a student for the world after school. It does not provide cultural capital to non-White students, and sometimes, not to the White students, either! It teaches students to conform or be punished, to be quiet and not take up too much room, and not speak up or out. That was every day for me as a young student in a private school.

I spent my entire educational career in private schooling. My elementary and secondary years were in parochial schools and my college years in a small church affiliated university. I understood that my continuation in the schools I attended for K–12 was contingent on my performance both behaviorally and academically. My responsibility was to uphold the school expectations, reputation, and promises of superior education. If I did not conform to the scripted language, values, dress, and behavior, my mother could be asked to find me a different educational environment. I may have been privileged in many ways, but I was also taught that I had a place and it was to be quiet, not take up too much room, and not to ever speak up or out unless it was sanctioned by the church. Control is control and it is seldom beneficial for the ones being controlled.

I have carried with me a feeling of being the odd human out since I first entered that second-grade classroom in the parochial school attached to the church we attended. My father had just passed away, my sister left for college, and my mom was working full time while raising five children. I was never able to find my niche in school, that sense of comfort or belongingness. I did not fit neatly into any category, or at least not the categories most of the other students fit into. I have conveyed this to my family many times over the years since but the environment in which I grew up was designed to be a distraction of sorts, a constant contradiction to my questioning of the people, motivations, and activity around me. It took me until adulthood and a purposeful re-examination to understand all of the implications of my educational experiences.

"A 'C' in this class is at least an 'A' in any public school," Mr. Green said, reviewing the syllabus in our sophomore AP English class and had just explained how difficult it was going to be for any of us to get high grades in his class. But, he promised, we would become proficient in literary analysis and excellent writers. His statement caused a complete paradigm shift for me. In that instant, I knew that even when the teacher is great (and he was), the values and words of authority should sometimes be questioned, preconceived ideas could be way off base, and thank goodness I wasn't having children because I'd be expected to send them to private Catholic school, and I wasn't going to do that. But I digress, let me explain how and why I came to remember that moment...

My large (by today's standards), lower middle class, White family lived in an all-White, very rural area and attended the local Catholic church long before I was born and long after I'd left the area after college. Our family friends were White and Catholic, and we were the only family in our immediate neighborhood (think more farm country, less HOA) that didn't attend the local public schools. My five siblings all attended Catholic school, as would I. Our parents sent us in order to pass along their religious beliefs. The schools attached to local churches were populated by an ordered hierarchy of priests, sisters (nuns), and a few lay teachers. The authority of the church and its representatives was to be respected and **never** questioned. Religion class was a part of the daily class cycle, with mass every Friday and on all Holy Days. Uniforms, which included plaid skirts for girls and dark blue dress pants for boys, designated sock colors and style, and shoe type, were worn by all students with no exceptions. Our words and actions, scripted within the handbook (Golann, 2021, p. 6) were overseen by the ever-present eyes of the church—and, as was often mentioned, the eyes of our omnipresent, omniscient God if no one else saw you. The environment was completely controlled. The culture was upheld by church expectations and everyone was to support it unreservedly. That was non-negotiable if you intended to remain in the school.

I'd always known that I did not learn from the same methods as the other students in my private school, but the education methods had been clear and set. I took longer than the other students to finish tests and work.

There was no additional reading assistance or individual help from teachers. After an initial group lesson, we were often expected to work alone. Parent-teacher conferences hadn't been pleasant and often ended with "She needs to apply herself," but I would regularly test very highly on standardized exams. One example is that I knew every word and action of the very stylized weekly Mass, but couldn't write the entire process down when tested in religion class. That was seen as refusal, lack of attention, or both and I nearly failed the class that year. I remained in the school but received little positive attention from my teachers. I began to find ways to help myself focus and finish work. I discovered that if I worked at a desk in the library with study walls or faced a corner, I was able to focus more closely on my work and I managed to graduate from eighth grade and be accepted into a parochial all-girls high school.

The high school was run by Catholic sisters and lay teachers, and we arrived each day from all over the greater metropolitan area. The majority of the 20 or so Black and Brown girls in our school of about 1,000 students were mostly not Catholic. They attended as an alternative to public school because the education and discipline were touted as superior, and often various need-based scholarships and benefactors paid their tuition. There was a distinct difference in the interactions of the teachers with those girls. Within the same space, faculty interaction with me might be a general question while the same information was solicited from Black students with an accusatory tone. Cultural capital was conveyed in a mismatched way for girls who looked like me, and not at all for the non-White young women.

The cognitive dissonance was difficult for two primary reasons. I had been told over and over to trust these teachers, that there was an innate goodness by virtue of their position and devotion to religious life, and that they were both my authority and my safe place. And also, that authority was to be respected and never questioned. But those experiences identified them as anything but a safe space for the Black students. I learned later that many of the students in the school were not Catholic, but the White non-Catholic girls typically came from wealthy families who were able to pay full tuition. I remember asking a group of non-Catholic friends why they endured daily religion class when they weren't Catholic. They said their parents told them to because it was better than going to public schools.

By this time, I'd ventured out and made friends with students from public schools in my neighborhood so I didn't understand that reasoning. Those students were progressing, those students had dreams and plans just as I did, and I conversed with them just as I did with my classmates. There was no real difference except our educational environments and the additional opportunities mine afforded me. And so, Mr. Green's statement will forever ring in my ears as a symbol of the mindset of those educators toward anyone who did not fit the expected mold or didn't look like the majority.

As it so happens, I did eventually have children, and I very mindfully did not send them to private schools. Instead, we embraced the diversity of the public schools as a gift.

My entire, very large extended family had all attended parochial schools through high school. I didn't know how to tell my mother about the decision to place our children in public schools and frankly was scared to do so. I knew it would be seen as not following the faith and not providing the best education available for them. But then that day came...

"Mrs. Sweeney, I need to talk to you about Sammy, I am very concerned for his safety."

I will never be able to forget that phone call. His teacher was genuinely concerned that my third grade son was significantly depressed and possibly considering hurting himself. Sam was struggling, really struggling. He understood concepts but struggled to put syllables together as he read. He avoided reading whenever possible but had a love for listening to stories that had begun when he was a toddler. He was a sweet, cherub-faced child with a sly grin, a love for singing and building, and big platinum-blond curls. His kindergarten and first-grade teachers enjoyed having him in class and kept telling me, "He's a little behind his peers, but he will catch up." I will admit that while I worried for my son, I knew my mother couldn't argue with the fact that he would not have fared well in parochial school. One less stressful situation.

Because he enjoyed experiences over reading so much, I exposed him and his younger brother to every hands-on opportunity I could find. Natural history museums, science centers, zoos, gardening, observatories, farms, Lego stores, nature centers, and history exhibits among many others. It wasn't until we moved and he switched schools that his second-grade teacher noted that he absorbed information like a sponge and could verbally teach a whole lesson on a topic but could not read at grade level. By third grade, it was quite evident that he understood the oral teaching and hands-on lessons, but he could not express himself in writing, and he still struggled to read at the appropriate level. He was falling behind. His imagination took him to wonderful worlds, and he could build and create from nearly any medium. We would orally quiz him before tests in various classes in preparation for school tests. He would do very well in that setting, but in the testing space, he would fail. The worst piece was when he recognized that he was behind his peers.

The process of evaluation and diagnosis of the problem was challenging. The school district hesitated and then finally stated that it would be another year before they could test Sam. There was no time. Sam's demeanor had changed completely and his behavior and interactions were withdrawn. I understood that the educators surrounding my child genuinely cared for him. It was a systemic issue that stood in the way. The district did not have the money or resources to quickly act on Sam's behalf. I informed the school that I would be having him privately assessed and would provide the results so long as they would then act upon them. They did. I again used my privilege and ability to quit work and focus on Sam. I worked with teachers, volunteered in the school several days a week, and was embraced as a team member in creating an educational environment he would thrive in.

   Shawn Tennent was a bright light at the end of a scary journey. In her resource room, she gently taught Sam through his fourth and fifth-grade years. She was a trained and licensed special education teacher with training in the Orton-Gillingham method. With her help, Sam learned how to decode and open written information for himself. And Shawn pulled him along in his writing as well. As he headed into Middle School, he was ready, with continued help, to tackle new subjects. I knew we had turned a corner when he wanted to buy books for himself at the scholastic book fair. I cried. I knew without any doubt that had he been in a parochial school, our experience would have been so different.

   Amid the educational challenges, Sam made friends and his group was more diverse than any I could have imagined at that age. I was thrilled with the exposure he received to so many people different in many ways from him. But I noticed a new issue. Our public school board was majority-ruled by parents whose students did not attend the public schools in the district. They attended parochial schools. In fact, they campaigned on that fact. What did private school parents want with the governing board of the public school system? Oh, my naivete.

Unveiling Truths: The Voucher Movement Does not Help Build Critical Consciousness

As chapter writing team members, we thought about what other extreme damage is happening due to this charter/voucher movement, we addressed the notion of critical consciousness. The concept of critical consciousness is important to discuss in relation to the question of how the charters/voucher movements recolonize because it provides a framework for understanding power dynamics, social justice, and the effects of educational policies on marginalized communities (Apple, 2006, 2019; Giroux, 2005; Hosford et al., 2019). When examining the charter/voucher movements, which involve expanding charter schools and using vouchers to fund private education, critical consciousness becomes relevant as charter systems are often criticized for their potential to exacerbate educational inequities and perpetuate social and economic divisions. This concept helps us understand how the charters/voucher movements may recolonize by analyzing their impacts on historically marginalized communities (as Hope is talking about) and allowing us to question the underlying motivations, power structures, and consequences of these educational policies. Before we delve into further discussion, it is important to understand what critical consciousness is.

Critical Consciousness

Critical consciousness, as conceptualized by Brazilian educator Paulo Freire, is a pedagogical approach aimed at liberating individuals from systemic inequities perpetuated by interdependent systems and institutions (Freire, 1973, 2017). It involves raising awareness and fostering a deep understanding of the social, economic, and cultural circumstances that shape people's lives, with the goal of empowering them to transform their reality (Prilleltensky, 1989). This process of achieving an illuminating awareness is not limited to recognizing one's own oppression but also understanding the oppressor's role in maintaining oppressive structures (Freire, 2017).

According to Freire, oppression dehumanizes both the oppressed and the oppressor, and critical consciousness serves as a pathway to reclaiming one's humanity by encouraging individuals to think critically about oppressive realities and challenge inequitable social conditions. It goes beyond passive acceptance of the status quo. It inspires individuals to become active agents of change, developing a critical understanding of the power dynamics that shape society and working towards dismantling oppressive systems through critical reflection and dialogue (Maton, 2008). The key outcome of critical consciousness is empowerment, which involves an active, participatory process where individuals and groups gain greater control over their identities and lives, protect human rights, and strive to reduce social injustice (Peterson, 2014). Through the development of critical consciousness, individuals become aware of their agency and the potential to challenge and transform oppressive systems, leading to personal and collective empowerment.

* * *

Lost in Transition: Rediscovering Belongingness in a Changing World

I (Tahreem Fatima) was raised in a small city in Pakistan. I am blessed with a very supportive family who has not just invested in me financially but emotionally, too. I completed my schooling years in a private school that was considered the best school in my hometown at that time. There are certain differences between public and private schools in Pakistan. The public schools are funded by the government and are notorious for their lack of resources, trained teachers, and quality of education. These schools have overcrowded classrooms and often face challenges due to budget constraints. Public schools follow the national curriculum, whereas private schools are famous for following international education systems, with examples that include the Cambridge or International Baccalaureate (IB) curriculum, although this situation is in the process of changing due to the recent introduction of the Single National Curriculum (SNC) in Pakistan.

The funding system of private schools is based on the tuition fee paid by parents or maybe some other resources of private funding, and this is the reason that students having lower socioeconomic backgrounds are enrolled in public schools as they are paying nothing or very low fees there. This situation could vary in different regions, though, as there are high and low-fee private schools based on better access to resources, libraries, and technologies. One notable difference which is very dear to the Pakistani public is private schools' prioritization of the English language in the classrooms, whereas public schools normally use local languages.

When I was studying at my school, students who spoke English were considered hardworking and successful. I was one of those students. My teachers often put me in charge of helping my classmates with their homework. I was a bright student and a favorite one to all my teachers. I have always considered this as my privilege. As I grew, I developed my interest in teaching. After finishing my schooling, I started helping students living in my neighborhood and opened a small tutoring center in my home. Most of the students I worked with attended private schools, but one was a public school student. I believe this was the time at which I began my career in teaching. My goal was to engage my students in understanding various concepts and their real-life applications. However, I still recall the concerns raised by students and their parents regarding the sole focus on achieving better grades and improving their English language skills. The only student attending a public school was an exceptionally brilliant fifth-grader, and he had a mother who wanted me to teach him at the level of private schools, hoping to secure his admission there in the future. His name was Zain.

Zain's mother normally picked him up late from our tutoring sessions, as she was a working woman. This never bothered me as I worked with this student. Outside of regular tutoring hours, Zain and I delved into subjects that surpassed the limitations of any prescribed syllabus, whether in public or private schools. He always had something to say about everything. I must admit that this student's level of critical awareness and ability to express himself for extended periods exceeded that of the students I served who went to private schools.

Unfortunately, Zain felt ostracized by the other students I was tutoring simply because he was from a public school. He was weak in spoken English, too, and I believe that was the only thing he struggled with. He often sat alone and quietly did his work. One day after the tutoring session, I asked him why he does not make friends, and he said, "I don't fit in with others—they study in big private schools—I have friends in my school, and I feel more confident with them." His words still bother me. Reflecting back on this whole story narrates one thing for sure: That in Pakistan there is no belongingness between those studying in public schools with those in private schools.

The charter/voucher movement is no different. As my friend and colleague Chiquita says, "Vouchers are the product of something even more devastating to a group—displacement, loss of sense of belongingness." The segregation is substantial, with private schools following standards mainly benefiting affluent families whose knowledge is perceived as superior (Sanders et al., 2018). It almost feels like the re-imposition of colonial values in the privatization of the schools, eroding students' critical consciousness. Now the question here to address is how students' critical consciousness is eroding.

When I (Tahreem) was completing the readings Dr. Poetter provided us for the course, I encountered many aspects that resonated with our problem. However, one particular aspect has proved to be connected and persistently troubling at the same time: The issue of charter schools' arrangements contributing to tribalism (Daly, 2022). As the movement caters to specific socioeconomic groups, this often results in schools with a relatively homogeneous student population. This homogeneity can have consequences on the development of critical consciousness as it limits exposure to diverse perspectives, cultures, and experiences that are crucial for fostering a well-rounded understanding of the world (Wright, 2000; Goodson, 2009). When a charter/voucher school predominantly enrolls students from a particular socioeconomic background, it creates an environment where students are more likely to interact with peers with similar social and economic circumstances. While it is natural for people to gravitate towards those who are similar to them, this lack of diversity can create a bubble-like environment that hinders the development of critical consciousness.

Diverse perspectives are essential for challenging preconceived notions, questioning the status quo, and developing a broader understanding of societal issues. Exposure to different perspectives fosters empathy, promotes critical thinking, and helps students navigate complex social and cultural landscapes. It allows them to engage in meaningful dialogue, appreciate different cultures, and develop a more nuanced understanding of social justice and equity (Au, 2012). In contrast, a lack of diversity can contribute to a limited worldview. Without exposure to different socioeconomic backgrounds, students may have limited knowledge about the challenges marginalized communities face or the systemic inequalities that exist in society (Anyon, 1981). This can result in a skewed understanding of social dynamics and a lack of empathy towards those who are different from them.

As I ponder the implications of this issue, I am reminded of the following quote:

> While public schools must adhere to federal civil rights protections, students using vouchers to attend private schools can be explicitly or implicitly denied opportunities based on their race and ethnicity, gender presentation, and disability.... Siphoning public dollars to fund private schools does not guarantee that all students will be admitted and adequately supported at private schools. (Resseger, 2023)

This quote emphasizes the fact that diverting public funds to support private schools does not ensure equal access or support for all students, as they may face discrimination based on various factors. The persistent issue of charter schools leading to tribalism and the reinforcement of inequalities has strengthened my resolve to advocate to promote critical consciousness among students. It is my life's purpose that education should not perpetuate divisions but should provide equal opportunities and nurture empathy among all students, regardless of their background. But it is obvious that this is not the mindset of the charter/voucher movement.

* * *

Misplaced Priorities

In this section, we criticize the charter/voucher system, which utilizes public funding to support privately-run schools, for its emphasis on privatization at the expense of fostering critical consciousness in students. Instead of prioritizing the empowerment of students through critical reflection and engagement with social realities, this system often focuses on market-driven competition and individual choice (Giroux, 2005; Hosford et al., 2019). Although the system may provide more educational options and promote improved outcomes through competition, this emphasis can divert attention away from nurturing critical consciousness. Privatized education prioritizes measurable academic results over developing students' critical thinking skills, social awareness, and engagement with broader societal issues.

Privatization in education is characterized by individual power, skills, and luck, whereas public education is rooted in civic rights, common responsibilities, and equal rights for all (Resseger, 2023). The charter/voucher system, emphasizing private choices, can seduce individuals with the allure of personal liberty and particular interests, but it fails to address the fundamental dilemma of the original social contract—the domination of the weak by the strong (Anyon, 1981, 2005, 2011). Again, this domination is evident in the segregation of students based on socioeconomic status, where the charter/voucher system perpetuates inequities and prevents the realization of critical consciousness, which involves recognizing and challenging systemic injustices (Freire, 2017).

Therefore, the charter/voucher system's prioritization of privatization over critical consciousness undermines the principles of equity and inclusion in education (Prilleltensky, 1989). The system's focus on private choices neglects the civic rights and common responsibilities associated with public education, leading towards the domination of powerful perspectives, which seems to be a contradiction to the common goals, and this is exactly the intent of colonization (Merriam-Webster Dictionary, n.d.). To address these concerns, it is crucial to reassess the impact of privatization and prioritize critical consciousness to promote equitable and inclusive education for all students.

Mindset of the System

Jacqlyn Schott, one of our doctoral colleagues, said the following while narrating her experience as a child studying in a system that puts a price on students' growth, emphasizing the profound effect it has had on her sense of self-worth and belonging:

> For a child who was born into a familial situation where she couldn't escape the trauma echoes deafening her to her own sense of self, worth, and belonging; for her White, single mother and her queer, Black babysitter-turned-grandma who wanted the best for her, no matter the sacrifice; for

the awakening she was able to find in the classroom and in a high school so celebrated for the arts that survived levy death knells; for the communities she still tries to build in classrooms of her own creation...for all the people and things still to come, I cannot fathom how different things would be had so many promises not come to fruition. Perhaps it's my unique relationship with trauma and all the oppressive systems inherent in it, but it sickens my soul learning the depths to which some will go just to line their pockets. Putting a price on growth, putting budgets on belonging, obfuscating truths with infectious lies that continue to take root and rot in our school systems...In a world where so many of our choices are taken away by rich, White, "Christian," cis-men, it's beyond tragedy how they continue to police and profitize (sometimes we need to make new words) Black and Brown bodies from their insidious, ignorant lack of critical consciousness.

The system of privatization prioritizes personal gain over the well-being and growth of individuals and communities. Our colleague here criticizes the practice of placing a price on growth and restricting belonging through budget constraints. She condemns the spread of lies and the manipulation of truth within school systems, suggesting that these falsehoods perpetuate oppressive systems. She also touches upon the intersectionality of oppression, specifically mentioning the actions of rich, White, "Christian," cisgender men. These individuals exercise control and profit from exploiting people of color, displaying a lack of critical consciousness. This passage reflects a call for awareness and action to challenge and dismantle oppressive systems. It highlights the importance of critical consciousness in recognizing and resisting these systems and underscores their impact on individuals' lives and communities, giving us hope for a better future.

Learning Where I am not Wanted

I (Chiquita) am from a small town in North Florida. I attended kindergarten at King High School, a K–12 predominantly Black school and beacon for the Black community. King was more than a school. It was a hub for gathering to celebrate community, culture, and to unify the community in resistance against racism and the Jim Crow Era that was ingrained in the city even after *Brown* and the Civil Rights Acts of the 1960s and 1970s. My grandmother, Mrs. Arriebelle White, would walk my brother and me to school in the morning because our parents were teachers at King and went in early. I was excited about school and enjoyed learning.

When I was six years old my world changed. I was forced to go to Baker Primary School across town in a White neighborhood. I had to ride a bus to get to school and my brother was sent to a different school. The burden of desegregating schools was never placed on White families. White families had choices. Black children had to disconnect from their communities and enter hostile territory. I could not walk and talk with Grandma as we went to school. I no longer felt the comfort of knowing that my brother, who was older than me, would check on me at school. And, he would not be waiting for me after school so we could meet Grandma. Our county in Florida was resistant to desegregation.

I can remember my first-grade teacher, Mrs. James, was unwelcoming. She stared down her glasses at the Black children in her room. When my eyes met hers, I knew she did not like me. She didn't like us. I had never had a White teacher before. Mrs. James made it known that she did not want to teach Black children. I learned early that she would not stop Barb from pinching me. Barb was the little White girl who sat next to me in class. When I pinched Barb back, I was sent to the principal's office. Our principal was Mr. Bell, who was the former principal of King High School. He was very tall and reassuring. Mrs. James would send me to his office each time I defended myself when Barb pinched or hit me. Mrs. James didn't know that Mr. Bell never punished me. He never gave me one consequence or paddling. Almost the same thing would occur each time Mrs. James sent me to the principal's office. Mrs. Ryle would say, "Hey, Little Hughes" and give me a pack of Lance cookies to eat. There were six cookies in the pack, they looked like Oreos. Afterwards, Mr. Bell would call me into his office and ask me what happened. He would say, "Uh huh." Then smile and look back at his desk and work on papers.

I sat in the chair across from him swinging my legs and finishing the Lance cookies Mrs. Ryle gave me. It was peaceful and comforting in his office. I wanted to stay with him all day but I knew he would have to send me back to class. By the time that I finished the last cookie, Mr. Bell would say, "Okay, time for you to go back to class." He didn't reprimand me or demand that I do better. He walked me to the office exit and watched as I walked down the sidewalk back to Mrs. James. When I got back to class, I remember being very quiet and having a sullen face. Mrs. James thought that I had been paddled. I could tell by her look that she was gloating in thinking that I was disciplined. That was not the case. I just didn't want to be in that space with her. I loved learning and the "place" called school. I was a good student, but I did not like Mrs. James because of how she made me feel. The message was, "We don't want you here." I wanted to go to my old school or at least stay with Mr. Bell.

Many times, I have reflected on Mr. Bell's actions with my parents. I am grateful for my mother and father, who would request parent/teacher meetings with any teacher who had a problem with teaching Black children. I am grateful for Mr. Bell. I have come to realize that he had to strike a delicate balance between active resistance, which could get him fired, and maintaining a position where he could be a refuge. He was safety and comfort for students like me who were dealing with the "Mrs. Jameses" of the world and the racism in integrated public school systems around the country.

The Residue

The residuals of the Jim Crow Era in our small southern town were not discussed and even to this day, there is a silence regarding these issues. For instance, de facto segregation still existed in communities, restaurants, and churches over 40 years after the Civil Rights Acts and more than 50 years after *Brown*. For instance, a well-known restaurant in my county was known for good seafood. However, it restricted the entrance of potential Black patrons using a one-way mirror and a buzzer. Only a select group have access; others are turned away. The door would open for White patrons. Black people were not welcomed, even after desegregation and the Civil Rights Acts of 1964 (Ulferts, 2001). Similarly, the voucher movement in America conveys the same discrimination that Black families experience at restaurants closed to them. And with the discrimination is a lack of critical consciousness to address the social injustices and subsequent oppression that arise when vouchers are used to segregate schools.

"The social meaning of racial segregation in the United States is the designation of a superior and an inferior caste, and segregation proceeds 'on the ground that colored citizens are...inferior and degraded'" (Matsuda, 2018, p. 59).

Brown v Board of Education (1954) may very well be the genesis of the widespread voucher movement in the United States. To desegregate schools marked the beginning of equality and the end of a caste system initiated through Jim Crow. Scholars have shown how *Brown* was a matter of interest convergence (Bell, 1980, 2018). Derrick Bell (1980) explains that racism is social and economic. Interest convergence means that White privilege or racism is not sacrificed when policies are passed to promote equality for Black and Brown people. This was most evident in the actions of Southern states before and after *Brown*.

School choice through vouchers is not a new phenomenon. In fact, the concept of neighborhood schools can be traced to the desegregation era when White families were allowed to open schools of choice in their communities to maintain segregated status (Ben-porath & Johanek, 2019; Hosford, et al., 2019; Welner et al., 2023). As a pre-emptive strike against the *Brown* ruling, legislatures in Alabama, Louisiana, Mississippi, Georgia, Virginia, North Carolina, and South Carolina created strategies that would preserve the status quo in White communities. Vouchers represented open opposition to federal overreach in the states' rights over education under the Constitution (Ben-porath & Johanek, 2019;, Hosford, et al., 2019; Welner et al., 2023). In South Carolina, local school boards were given the authority to create attendance boundaries. To preserve White supremacy and segregation, Mississippi provided funding for White parents to choose private schools and avoid desegregation. Georgia passed laws to defund schools that desegregated and Governor Vandiver ran an effective gubernatorial campaign by promising White parents relief from desegregation (Welner et. al., 2023).

Even in the evolution of vouchers from the 1950s to now, the seminal argument is that the "parent has the right to buy the educational service he deems best for his child" (Brady, 1954 in Welner et al., 2023, p. 34). Increasingly, parents are being sold on the value of social capital in school settings. Therefore, they use the power of choice to facilitate selective, lifelong social networks for their children and as a vehicle for their children to gain upward mobility within the social hierarchy (Hosford et. al., 2019). Parental choice is an impetus behind the voucher movement. In plain language, vouchers are educational currency and serve as a medium of exchange for parental rights over school choice (Hosford et. al., 2019). Perhaps, what has been most egregious in the voucher movement are the economic, educational, and social inequalities caused to vulnerable communities through district-based attendance policies. "What reason have the black and very poor to lend their credence to a market system that has proved so obdurate and so resistant to their pleas at every turn" (Kozol, 1991, p. 76).

In the reality of vouchers, Black and Brown students and families absorb most of the negative consequences economically, socially, and geographically (Wright et. al., 2020). This strategy has resurfaced even more strongly in this era of vouchers and the privatization of education.

Nothing seems to matter to us until it begins to hit closer to home. The complexities of the situation demand a closer view of the systems that are intertwined to build the compulsory inequities. The voucher movement is no different. My colleague, Hope, explains that vouchers are the product of something even more devastating to a group—displacement, loss of sense of belongingness. The more I think about this, it is evident that there is a strategic, oppressive tactic to dismantle and displace Black and Brown communities. The sagas of Chicago Public Schools, New Orleans, and Detroit Public Schools seemed distant until the past decades have proven we have succumbed to the neoliberalism wave (Welner et. al., 2023; Wright et. al., 2020; Zernike, 2016). Now we see the same unfolding in cities like Cincinnati. It's dollars and cents, power and politics, and less common sense.

Neighborhood schools are becoming browner and poorer (Hosford et al., 2019). America is majority White but our public schools are majority Black and Brown. Less than 20% of White students attend urban schools, and over 80% of White students are distributed across suburban and rural schools (Colomo, 2013). The American dream is becoming more distant for Black and Brown families. The rising cost of homes places home ownership out of reach of many residents in Cincinnati who were hoping to finally end many years of renting. What do houses have to do with this? Taxes, through levies, support municipalities and are the locally required effort that is used to fund police departments, volunteer fire departments, libraries, hospitals, and, last but not least, schools. It can be said that police departments, hospitals, and fire departments belong to the citizenry. Likewise, we should be able to say the same for schools. Consequently, this is not always the case. Schools are publicly funded and privately segregated. Schools should belong to their neighborhoods.

Recolonizing Communities, Resegregating Schools

Neoliberalist ideologies blame teachers, parents, and students for failing schools (Hosford et. al., 2019). Observing the profitable opportunity, corporations and wealthy venture capitalists are funding special schools that are presented as innovative programs. To put it bluntly, these efforts reflect the resegregating colonization of schools and the recolonization of communities into the proverbial "haves and have nots" (Apple, 2006; Hosford et. al., 2019). School boards and state education agencies cannot compete with the power, politics, and seemingly inexhaustible money coffers of venture philanthropists (big money) like the Broad Foundation, The Waltons, and Bill Gates. Recolonization is oppressive, negatively affecting neighborhood schools and the economies of Black and Brown communities. We have seen it in Philadelphia and Detroit. Recolonization is the product of a process in urban development and planning where fewer resources are given to poor communities called divestment. Cities discontinue resources that include such things as grants for homeowner repairs, tax incentives, and access to services that are necessary for a high quality of life (McCullough et al., 2022). Over time, businesses relocate causing the loss of jobs, services, and funds necessary to sustain amenities within the community. Homeowners lose equity in their property. This is the beginning of gentrification.

According to McCullough et al. (2022), gentrification is the process of economic revitalization in lower-income communities. In most cases, communities whose members were mostly Black and Brown residents experience demographic changes and become Whiter, younger, and more middle to upper class (Thurber et al., 2019; Whitlow, 2023). Older structures that have declined in value are torn down and new structures erected. Homes that are sold below market value are flipped, renovated, and resold at a higher value.

Property equity is a form of economic power. The value of your home builds wealth and can be used to borrow money. However, when there is a decline in property values, those who can are forced to sell their homes below market value and leave the neighborhood. Some walk away from the debt. It's like a real-life game of monopoly. The investors increase their property portfolios and rent and housing prices increase. Those who cannot leave are forced to stay in impoverished conditions. And it has happened and continues to happen all around the US, especially in Black and Brown communities. Why? The residents of these communities do not possess political and economic power privileged through third and fourth generation wealth and property ownership. Property owners have a voice in the local economy and that voice allows them to enjoy certain amenities in exchange for the support they give to schools and local economies. People who do not own property have less economic and political power to advocate for their needs. And without a voice, these communities are deemed expendable. As with the cities of Detroit, New York, and Philadelphia, the goal is to attract a large number of wealthier residents and revitalize the economy. Proponents claim that gentrification boosts economic growth, increases property values and neighborhood amenities, reduces crime and makes neighborhoods safer (McCullough, 2022; Pearman et al., 2020).

The surface view of gentrification includes beautiful modern apartment homes with condominiums lining the streets. New businesses are attracted to the revitalization and home sales increase. In Cincinnati, the scenery in several urban communities reflects economic growth and prosperity. Gentrification has been summarized as "a back-to-the-city movement by capital rather than people" (Whitlow, 2023, p. 1101).

In contrast, there is an ugly side of gentrification which makes it easy to recolonize communities and to support charters and private schools. When wealthier families move into gentrified neighborhoods, existing residents are displaced. Older citizens and lower SES families with school-aged children are forced to leave and find affordable housing. Gentrification causes housing insecurity along with psychosocial trauma (Croff et. al., 2021; Largent et. al., 2020). There is a trickle-down effect on schools. Student mobility is a symptom of housing insecurity and sometimes families become homeless. Many of the urban neighborhood schools suffer from declining enrollment, while struggling to close the historical achievement gap due to funding inequities.

As Hope alluded to earlier, there is displacement which causes "root shock," a type of disorientation caused because residents lose cultural associations, businesses, and familiar landmarks. There is a loss of social networks and human connectedness, which results in stress and anxiety: "...displacement creates emotional and psychological wounds that are difficult to heal and inflicts trauma that is often undiagnosed among individuals as community bonds are torn apart" (McCullough et al., 2022, p. 24).

The new property owners (who can afford a higher tax base) have little interest in supporting neighborhood schools. This brings me back to Tahreem's discourse on critical consciousness and the distractions that keep people from questioning the motives behind the new school. Charter schools are opening right down the street, promising to provide a better education for students who are living through existing economic, social, and educational inequalities. School transportation boundaries have been redrawn to support gentrification and vouchers.

Zain is Jamal

As Tahreem writes about Zain, I (Chiquita) am considering the many children in the U.S. like Zain who are and have been penalized because of the families to which they have been born. I am reflecting on the Zains that I have encountered in my career and those with whom I am associated with at this very moment. Every child deserves to learn without being judged for their geographical location, the zip code that denotes the socio-economic status. In Cincinnati, Zain is Jamal. Jamal lives in an urban neighborhood and attends the neighborhood school which is 66% minority. His school is Jacob Peace Preparatory Elementary (JPP). Jamal has been attending JPP since preschool. He is going to the second-grade next year. Two older siblings are also attending JPP in 5th and 6th grades and a younger sibling will start preschool in Fall 2023. Jamal's parents are pleased with his progress. JPP has a Global Citizens Science Program that provides opportunities for students to address real-world problems and participate in creating community solutions through project-based learning. Jamal's mother says the school has a welcoming atmosphere and a sense of belongingness and community. Jamal's family lives less than two blocks from the school. His mother and father take turns walking their children to school and can return home in time for the commute to work. If the school board's proposal is approved, JPP will become a grades 3–8 school. Jamal and his younger brother will attend the new preschool.

Before the neighborhood began to change, Jamal's parents had the assurance and convenience of knowing their children were together at the end of school and less than two blocks from their home. The new primary school is at least two miles away. Jamal's mother does not want her smaller children on buses with older students. In addition, the newly renovated homes have caused an increase in property taxes, making Jamal's parents consider selling their home and moving to a more affordable community. They would need to rent as housing prices are out of reach for them. Next year, Jamal's parents are not sure how to prepare for their children's school attendance, a new neighborhood with fewer amenities, and the family's new economic situation. They decided to attend a community meeting where other residents have gathered to confront what seems to be the resegregation of their neighborhood and the increase of funding for charter schools.

For JPP, the charter school competition is not from private funders but from the local school board who has acquiesced to market-based strategies as a strategy to recruit and retain students of an upper socioeconomic status. The resulting action promises an increase in funding through tax levies. Board meetings have centered around the restructuring of elementary schools for the opening of a new preschool that would serve grades Pre-K–2. However, there is a contingent of watchful citizens who have been spurred by conspicuously familiar patterns. A level of critical consciousness has emerged among parents, community members who are making their voices known during live Board meetings broadcast and recorded on Youtube. During one Board meeting, a veteran teacher at JPP called out the district for creating a new school to appease wealthier White parents rather than requiring those students to attend the existing neighborhood school. The teacher explained that the efforts give the appearance of resegregation as the newer school has a smaller percentage of demographically diverse students although many of its students share the same residential streets as students zoned for the neighborhood school.

Tell Me Where You Live, I'll Tell You About Your School

"Tell me where you live and I'll tell you who you are: how good your school is, how freely drugs flow, what your future potential looks like, how likely you are to live to full adulthood, what you imagine you can accomplish, if you still have an imagination left at all" (McCullough et al., 2022, p. 34).

In the context of recolonization, there is a relationship between school zones, economic power, and property ownership. The influence of money and power draws squiggly lines. School districts seemingly relieve politicians from making the demarcation for congressional districts. House values are determined by zip codes, communities, and boundary lines. The lines are not always clear, concise, and straight as one would imagine. Neighborhood streets are gerrymandered to protect and increase ownership equity for affluent tax payers as well as accommodate their school preferences. While redlining is illegal in real estate transactions, the practice still exists covertly through school choice and vouchers.

School performance informs home sales. Attendance boundaries are means for ascribing value to people, places, and property. Communities are recolonized by factors that are associated with attendance boundaries, school performance, and parent views of the school. Higher home values have been associated with higher performing schools (Bucerius et. al., 2017; Danielson et al., 2015). Economically resourced parents with school-aged children are willing to pay more so that their children have a good education and greater opportunities. Conversely, parents who have been displaced by gentrification live in neighborhoods that lack the economic power to improve educational opportunities for their children. Scholars problematize that negative impacts are mostly felt by communities of color via zip code colonization (McCullough et al., 2022), forced inequality through school choice and privatization (Apple, 2006; Giroux, 2005), health disparity and the loss of social support and networks, especially for children and older citizens (Pearman, 2019), and cultural erasure where wealthy elites rename or discard symbolic artifacts that embodied identity and historical value (Thurber et al., 2021).

We are in an era where inequality is weaponized. Vouchers are "repurposed" weapons in the arsenal of neoliberals and policy makers who want to privatize education using market-driven approaches. Vouchers provide a legal avenue for the miseducation of children.

School vouchers divert public funds from public schools and create private tuition to specialized, and many times, substandard educational environments (Dyer & Reedy, 2022). This whole concept of choice and parents' rights is a facade to create policies that legalize inequality. Billed as an alternative to failing schools, vouchers have many negative consequences, including the exclusion of Black and Brown families, the disenfranchising of neighborhoods, and silencing the voices of communities of color (Wright et. al., 2020). Vouchers have been viewed as an existential threat to public schools. On the surface, school vouchers are designed as a solution for families whose students were forced to attend (sometimes according to zip code) chronically failing schools. In an era of inequality and social injustice in schools, what is evident is that vouchers are just one scheme in a market-driven approach to resegregate public education and dismantle public schools (Giroux, 2005; Hosford et. al., 2019; Sanders et. al., 2018).

Breaking Boundaries: Reimagining Possibilities

Critical consciousness motivates us to break boundaries and question the status quo to imagine new possibilities. Our approach to writing this piece was to draw on critical consciousness to establish the historical contention between vouchers and the threat posed to ensuring equality in public education for all students. We decided that the best interests of readers would be served by transparency as we provided personal narratives of our experiences in education. I, Chiquita, have experienced the hostility of racism in public education although I loved the place called school. My colleague, Hope, recalls how her private schooling did not provide a realistic view of the world for which she would live. In similar fashion, my colleague, Tahreem, learned that when students from lower-income families are disconnected from their communities they can feel displaced, losing their sense of belongingness. The diversity of our life journeys strengthens our alliance in support of public education. We want to reiterate that vouchers are tools of inequality, used to segregate and recolonize communities, bringing about unequal outcomes for students. Vouchers reify separatist thinking about education.

Hope's parents chose her private educational setting and their actions planted seeds of bias which were difficult for her to reconcile. Drawing from her own personal experiences, Hope ensured that her children were exposed to and learned appreciation for diversity. JPP, as a neighborhood school, reflects the social, historical and cultural connections of the community, which is comforting for Jamal and his parents. I appreciated the connections I made when King was my school. But the new school included teachers like Mrs. James whose discriminatory behaviors created unnecessary stress for students entering a new learning environment. Belongingness is an essential part of the school learning experience.

Zain deserved a high-quality education just like Tahreem was receiving, except Tahreem was in private school. Both Tahreem and Zain should have been confident in receiving an excellent education from their public schools. Divestment in public schools breeds unequal educational outcomes. Gentrification and vouchers destroy the bonds which are vital to the quality of life for students and families.

We must use critical consciousness to guide our decisions and to liberate us from the biases that hinder our abilities to engage in activism for the good of humanity. We will not conclude this discussion on a note that appears to be hopeless. For we believe that public education is the agent for developing democratic citizenship and is a public good. In fact, it is the one minimal asset to which all Americans have the right of immediate ownership. Therefore, we offer fuel for thought and action to parents, teachers, students, and community members. We use the power of written words to center and uplift those who have been marginalized and colonized.

References

Abrams, S. E., & Koutsavlis, S. J. (2023). *The Fiscal Consequences of Private School Vouchers.*

Anyon, J. (1981). Social class and school knowledge. *Curriculum Inquiry, 11*(1), 3–42. https://doi.org/10.2307/1179509

Anyon, J. (2005). What "counts" as educational policy? Notes toward a new paradigm. *Harvard Educational Review, 75*(1), 65–88.

Anyon, J. (2011). *Marx and education.* New York, NY: Routledge.

Apple, M. W. (2006). Understanding and interrupting neoliberalism and neoconservatism in education pedagogies. *An International Journal, 1*(1), 21–26. https://doi.org/10.1207/s15544818ped0101_4

Apple, M. W. (2019). On doing critical policy analysis. *Educational Policy, 33*(1), 276–287. https://doi.org/10.1177/0895904818807307

Au, W. (2012). *Critical curriculum studies: Education, consciousness, and the politics of knowing.* Routledge.

Bell, D. A. (2018). *Faces at the bottom of the well.* Basic Books.

Bell, D. A. (1980). *Brown v. Board of Education* and the interest-convergence dilemma. *Harvard Law Review, 93*(3), 518–533.

Ben-Porath, S. R., & Johanek, M. C. (2019). *Making up our mind: What school choice is really about.* University of Chicago Press.

Blakemore, E. (2021, May 3). Colonialism facts and information. *Culture.* https://www.nationalgeographic.com/culture/article/colonialism#:~:text=Colonialism%20is%20defined%20as%20%E2%80%9Ccontrol,cultural%20values%20upon%20its%20people

Bucerius, S. M., Thompson, S. K., & Berardi, L. (2017). "They're colonizing my neighborhood": (Perceptions of) social mix in Canada. *City & Community, 16*(4), 486–505.

Butzin, S. (1997). Whatever happened to project CHILD? *Learning & Leading with Technology, 24*(6), 24–27.

Christian Hauser, W. (2023, March 13). *Parents upset after charter school announces closure at the end of the school year.* WKRC. https://local12.com/news/local/parents-upset-after-charter-school-announces-closure-halfway

-through-the-school-year-citizens-world-charter-school-staff-shutting-down-building-classrooms-class-schools-enroll-madisonville-cincinnati-ohio

Cowen, Josh. (2023, February 21). *School vouchers: There is no upside | Shanker Institute.* https://www.shankerinstitute.org/blog/school-vouchers-there-no-upside

Coloma, R. S. (2020). Decolonizing urban education. *Educational Studies, 56*(1), 1–17. https://doi.org/10.1080/00131946.2019.1711095.

Croff, R., Hedmann, M., & Barnes, L. L. (2021). Whitest city in America: A smaller Black community's experience of gentrification, displacement, and aging in place. *The Gerontologist, 61*(8), 1254–1265.

Danielsen, B. R., Fairbanks, J. C., & Zhao, J. (2015). School choice programs: The impacts on housing values. *Journal of Real Estate Literature, 23*(2), 207–232.

Daly, L. (2022, December 6). Re-contextualizing how i view public education: an exploration of the Ohio Coalition for Equity & Adequacy of School Funding. *Ohio Archives.* Retrieved June 20, 2023 from https://sites.ohio.edu/library-archives-blog/2022/12/06/oceasf-exploration

Davis, G. S. (2004). Roman catholicism: Theology and colonization. In G. P. Fernandez (Ed.), *Encyclopedia of religion and war* (pp. 384–390). Routledge.

Dyer, S., & Reedy, M. (2022). The promised education movement. *Columbus Bar Lawyers Quarterly,* 30–37.

Finn, C. E. (2016, May 9). Where did charter schools come from? *Education Next.* https://www.educationnext.org/where-did-charter-schools-come-from

Fisher, D. R. (n.d.). *Education in the Settler Colony: Displacement, inequality, and disappearance via charter schools.*

Freire, P. (1973). *Education for critical consciousness.* Seabury Press.

Freire, P. (2017). *Pedagogy of the oppressed.* Penguin Classics.

Golann, J. W. (2021). *Scripting the moves: Culture and control in a "no-excuses" charter school.* Princeton University Press.

Goodson, I. (2009). Personal history and curriculum study. In E. Short & L. Waks (Eds.), *Leaders in curriculum studies: Intellectual self-portraits* (pp. 91–104). Sense.

Giroux, H. A. (2005). The terror of neoliberalism: Rethinking the significance of cultural politics. *College Literature, 32*(1), 1–19.

Horsford, S. D., Scott, J. T., & Anderson, G. L. (2019). *The politics of education policy in an era of inequality: Possibilities for democratic schooling.* Routledge.

Heubert, J. P. (1997). *Schools without rules? Charter schools, federal disability law, and the paradoxes of deregulation.* Harvard Project on Schooling and Children, Cambridge, MA.

Knight-Abowitz, K., & Karaba, R. (2020). What is a public education and why we need it: A philosophical inquiry into self-development, cultural commitment, and public engagement (Walter Feinberg). *Philosophical Inquiry in Education, 24*(1), 115–119. https://doi.org/10.7202/1070561ar

Kozol, J. (1991). *Savage inequalities*. Crown.

Largent, A., & Quimby, M. (2020). Gentrification, displacement, and perception of community among longtime residents of Austin, Texas: Implications from six case studies. *Journal of Integrated Social Sciences, 10*(1), 52–85.

Lipman, P. (2015). Capitalizing on crisis: Venture philanthropy's colonial project to remake urban education. *Critical Studies in Education, 56*(2), 241–258. https://doi.org/10.1080/17508487.2015.959031

Lubienski, C., Brewer, T. J., & Malin, J. (2023). Bait and switch: How voucher advocates shift policy objectives. In K. Welner, G. Orfield, & L. Huerta (Eds.), *The school voucher illusion: Exposing the pretense of equity* (pp. 127–147). Teachers College Press.

Maton K. I. (2008). Empowering community settings: agents of individual development, community betterment, and positive social change. *American Journal of Community Psychology, 41*(1–2), 4–21. https://doi.org/10.1007/s10464-007-9148-6

Matsuda, M. J. (2018). *Words that wound: Critical race theory, assaultive speech, and the first amendment*. Routledge.

McCullough, C. R., Datts, K., Allen-Handy, A., Sterin, K., & Escalante, K. (2022). Zip code colonization: Counter-narratives of gentrification's traumatic impact on Philadelphia's Black educational communities. *Journal of Trauma Studies in Education, 1*(3), 23–44.

Pearman, F. A. (2020). Gentrification, geography, and the declining enrollment of neighborhood schools. *Urban Education, 55*(2), 183–215.

Peterson N. A. (2014). Empowerment theory: clarifying the nature of higher-order multidimensional constructs. *American Journal of Community Psychology, 53*(1–2), 96–108. https://doi.org/10.1007/s10464-013-9624-0

Prilleltensky, I. (1989). Psychology and the status quo. *American Psychologist, 44*(5), 795–802. https://doi.org/10.1037/0003-066X.44.5.795

Pont, C. du. (n.d.). *Research guides: colonization, decolonization and postcolonialism: An interdisciplinary guide: Key concepts*. Retrieved June 7, 2023, from https://libguides.uwinnipeg.ca/c.php?g=392214&p=2664087

Resseger, J. (2023, April 18). *A tsunami of private school tuition vouchers at public schools' expense: Is there anything we can do?* [web log]. Retrieved June 20, 2023, from https://janresseger.wordpress.com/2023/04/18/37904/

Sanders, R., Stovall, D., & White, T. (2018). *Twenty-first-century Jim Crow schools: The impact of charters on public education*. Beacon Press.

Tebben, S. (2022, December 8). Private school voucher expansion will bring about school choice, Ohio GOP sponsor says. *Ohio Capital Journal*. https://ohiocapitaljournal.com/2022/12/08/private-school-voucher-expansion-will-bring-about-school-choice-ohio-gop-sponsor-says/

Thurber, A., Krings, A., Martinez, L. S., & Ohmer, M. (2021). Resisting gentrification: The theoretical and practice contributions of social work. *Journal of Social Work, 21*(1), 26–45.

Ulferts, A. (2021, February 17). Race relations at the crossroads. *Tampa Bay Times.* https://www.tampabay.com/archive/2001/02/17/race-relations-at-the-crossroads/

Welner, K., Orfield, G., & Huerta, L. A. (Eds.). (2023). *The school voucher illusion: Exposing the pretense of equity.* Teachers College Press.

Whitlow, J. (2019). Gentrification and countermovement: The right to counsel and New York City's affordable housing crisis. *Fordham Urban Law Journal, 46*(5), 1081–1136.

Wright, H. K. (2000). Nailing Jell-O to the wall: Pinpointing aspects of state-of-the-art curriculum theorizing. *Educational Researcher, 29*(5), 4–13.

Wright, J., Whitaker, R., Muhammad, K., & Briscoe, F. (2020). The color of neoliberal reform: A critical race policy analysis of school district takeovers in Michigan. *Urban Education 55*(3), 424–447. https://doi.org/10.1177/0042085918806943

Zernike, K. (2016, May 9). New Orleans Plan: Charter Schools, With a Return to Local Control. *The New York Times.* https://www.nytimes.com/2016/05/10/us/charter-driven-gains-in-new-orleans-schools-face-a-big-test.html

3

Follow the Money

Tailyn Walborn
Carolyn S. Craig
Dongxia Sang

> *It's raining in the library, there's puddles in the halls. There's coal dust in my textbooks, and you could punch holes in these walls. But the state ain't got the money to fix up this old school, so I'm going to the next county and jump in their olympic pool.*
> —The Ballad of Nathan DeRolph (from Daly, 2022)

When we began to outline this chapter as a writing team, I (Tailyn) started to struggle. There was no question in my mind that the voucher system's fiscal impact on public schools is important, and I agreed with my group that it's necessary to show the numbers, but how do we do this using the currere method? How do I, as a doctoral student with no personal ties to private schools or voucher programs, take an autobiographical approach to reflecting on how vouchers undermine public education? The answer was there, but I couldn't seem to grasp it. It took forgetting our established objectives, procedures, and timeline, and just writing the thoughts that had been flowing in my mind since the inception of my interest in public school finance to realize that my feelings on the matter are personal. They are a result of my story. They are part of who I am, and where I've come from.

I (Tailyn) didn't attend a wealthy school district, but we had access to College Prep, Advanced Placement, College Credit Plus, and even Career-Technical Education, so that everyone had a variety of opportunities after graduation. It never occurred to me that there were districts who had more. Worse, it never occurred to me that there were districts who had far less. As a child growing up, it's hard to understand that disparities and inequities abound, and even harder to understand that this is something certain people actually work to promote on a daily basis.

Our country has seen more division over the past decade than I ever thought possible. Stories I see in the news, behavior seen on the streets, and proposed policies by politicians often feel as though they come out of some dystopian novel that Mr. Johns would have made us read in AP English. But these things aren't works of fiction, and some proposed policies we are seeing at the state level have terrifying implications for the future of our society.

Horace Mann, often known as the father of American education, believed that education is a public good that should be paid for with public funding so that all citizens have equal access to this resource:

> The distance between the two extremes of society is lengthening, instead of being abridged. With every generation, fortunes increase on the one hand, and some new privation is added to poverty on the other. We are verging towards those extremes of opulence [wealth] and of penny [poverty], each of which unhumanizes the mind... The spread of education, by enlarging the cultivated class or caste, will open a wider area over which the social feelings will expand, and, if this education should be universal and complete, it would do more than all things else to obliterate [erase] distinctions in society. (Mann, 1848, as quoted in Caggia, n.d.)

More directly "education, then, beyond all other devices of human origin, is the great equalizer of conditions of men (sic),–the balance wheel of the social machinery" (Mann, 1848, as quoted in Caggia, n.d.). And yet, we are currently faced with the reality that certain people are trying to defund our public education system. Were it to provide fair and equitable educational opportunities to all, I'd say a conversation is worth having, but the numbers don't lie. With the threat of universal vouchers (they will have already come to Ohio by the time this work is published) and an increasing number of publicly funded private schools and charter schools, the already underfunded public school system is losing money to private enterprise.

What's Happening With Vouchers?

To understand what's going on, I believe it is important to have a basic understanding of the public school funding model in Ohio, as well as some recent numbers. Ohio public schools receive funding from four major sources, which, for the 2020–2021 school year, included approximately 41% state funding; 43% local funding; 9% federal funding; and 7% other non-tax funding (Thomas B. Fordham Institute, 2023, p. 68). During this same time, total Ohio public school spending per-pupil ranged from $12,050-$15,021, with the average being just over $13,000 (Thomas B. Fordham Institute, 2023, p.72), which is far less than some other states, but that's a discussion for another time.

According to the FY2022 District Profile Report, released by the Ohio Department of Education, of the 606 public school districts reported, 594 received less than this average in state funds (Ohio Department of Education, 2022B). Based on the average breakdown of revenue stated above, where 41% came from the state, with an average per pupil spending of $13,000, all schools should receive at least $5,330 per pupil from the state. These schools are then responsible for making up the difference between what they are receiving from state, federal, and other non-tax funds, and what it actually costs per pupil, through local funding, which is raised through property taxes.

This issue has been at the center of a decades-long debate on whether Ohio's public school funding model is equitable (see *DeRolph v. State*), with the Supreme Court of Ohio ruling that the system "fails to provide for a thorough and efficient system of common schools" (*DeRolph v. Board of Education*, 1997, p. 4), which has resulted in four different school funding models in the past 17 years (Churchill, 2021, para. 1). Unfortunately, all of these models still rely heavily on the local school districts' property values. Although the state claims they take this into consideration when determining the base funding they provide to each district, they are providing what they consider sufficient for an *adequate* education, a term that is difficult to define, and is often considered too low to provide fair educational opportunity to all students (Sweetland, 2014), especially with the responsibility for making up the difference resting on the individual locales.

Ohio has an established minimum tax rate for localities to raise funds for their districts. Beyond this, districts can pass levies to increase this tax rate. Within these two sentences lie the largest issues with Ohio's public school funding model. First, an established minimum tax rate doesn't guarantee equitable, or even equal funds for all districts. If you have a district that contains high-income housing, that district will receive a higher dollar amount than a lower-income district, regardless of school-district expenditures. Additionally, relying heavily on levies places the financial burdens of our schools in the hands of our citizens, some of whom can't afford higher taxes, and others who feel disconnected to the school system, often voting down levies and issues, resulting in even wider disparities in local funding. To put this in perspective, in 2020–2021, the amount per pupil collected through local revenue in Ohio ranged from $1,386.20 to $22,915.03 (Ohio Department of Education, 2022B).

When a student decides to utilize the EdChoice program's scholarship vouchers to pay for a charter school or homeschooling or a fully private education, not only are the public schools losing the minimal amount of state funding they would have received per pupil, as Dyer and Reedy (2022) highlight, "the amount deducted for charters (and to a lesser extent, vouchers) was almost always *more* than the student would have received from the state if they had remained in the local public school" (p. 33). They continue on to explain this with a simplified example:

> ...let's say the state says it should cost $100 to educate a student in XYZ school district. But the state expects the district to pick up half that cost using local revenue. So, the state would send $50 to educate the student and XYZ would raise local revenue to cover the remaining amount. However, if that same student decided to go to a charter school, the state would transfer $100 to the charter school to cover the student's costs, even though the state would have provided half that cost to the local school district. (p. 33)

In reality, the numbers can be far worse. In his article on educating politicians about the impact of vouchers on public schools, Hemminger (2023) points out that "Ohio's expanded voucher program provides $5,500 per student in grades kindergarten through eighth grade and $7,500 for grades 9–12" (para. 9). Additionally, charter school students receive, on average, $9,066 in state aid (Dyer & Reedy, 2022, p .34). Hemminger (2023) continues, "by comparison, Mohawk [a public school district in Northwest Ohio] receives just $1,987 per pupil from the state. Private or charter schools receive four times the state funding per pupil" (para. 9), and this is bound to increase.

According to the Ohio Department of Education (2021), "in fiscal year (FY) 2021, the state of Ohio spent more on primary and secondary education than at any other time in state history. And state education spending will continue to increase" (para. 1). Notice that this statement doesn't imply that they are referring to just public school funding. Not only are these school choice options taking funding away from our public schools, they are draining our tax dollars at a faster rate per-pupil, and some can even take tax dollars for students who were never supported by public school funding. In the first place, the majority of students receiving vouchers in some of the more prominent school choice states, including as many as two thirds from the state of Ohio, were never attending public schools to begin with (Dyer & Reedy, 2022, p. 36). "By giving state-funded vouchers to families who already have access to and can afford private school, homeschooling, and other educational costs, revenues that states could have spent on public education *and other critical services* [emphasis added] are reduced over time" (Hinh, 2023, p. 3).

The voucher program is not only a movement toward privatization, it is defunding our public education system. It is mind blowing that voucher program advocates don't see a problem with giving private enterprises quadruple the amount of funding in state tax dollars than we are giving our public schools. Additionally, despite receiving a substantial amount of state funds, these schools do not adhere to the same oversight and accountability as public schools. In fact, a 2015 article released by the *Akron Beacon Journal* revealed that charter schools were misspending state funds "nearly four times more often than any other type of taxpayer-funded agency" (*Akron Beacon Journal*, 2015, para. 2). Charter schools also have lower test scores and graduation rates than public schools, and spend almost double on administrative costs (Dyer & Reedy, 2022, p. 30). Finally, to emphasize the injustice of these misappropriated funds, Dyer and Reedy (2022) found that, of the $100 million the Electronic Classroom of Tomorrow (ECOT) received one year, all but just $2,000 came from public school districts who outperformed them (p. 35). This is the same ECOT that in June of 2022, was found by the Ohio Auditor of State to owe more than $117 million that it stole from the state by reporting inflated numbers and fake students (Ohio Auditor of State, 2022, para. 1), and "over a 15-year period likely was paid one half billion dollars for students claimed, but not educated" (Phillis, 2023B, para. 2).

What's even more concerning is how Ohio's EdChoice budget continues to expand. What was created under the ruse of helping low-income families trapped in "failing schools," charter schools and vouchers have cost us over $18.6 billion, which includes $361 million for vouchers for just the 2021–2022 school year (Calderone, 2023, para. 1; Dyer and Reedy, 2022, p. 35). In fact, the typical private schools receiving these funds aren't the elite schools we often hear about in the media; instead, they are small "sub-prime" institutions, who often open their doors just long enough to receive funding, much like, as Cowen (2023) points out, fraudulent small businesses emerged to receive PPP Covid relief funds (para. 11).

Administrators now fear that the continued expansion of these programs will cut into necessary funds for the Fair School Funding Plan, which was created in response to the DeRolph rulings (Hancock, 2023, para. 11). The framework of the Fair School Funding Plan (FSFP) consists of multiple components summarized by Churchill (2021). Base funding is determined by a new model, and is then multiplied by the state share percentage (SSP), which compensates for property values and resident income, providing more state dollars to districts less able to generate revenue. There are also targeted assistance funds available for poorer districts. Transportation funding is based on per-mile or per-pupil costs, and can be adjusted by SSP. Additionally, funding is available based on the following add-ons: students with disabilities, economically disadvantaged, career-technical education, gifted education, and English learners, all of which can be adjusted by the SSP with the exception of economically disadvantaged, which is adjusted by its own variable. Finally, there are guaranteed funds available to ensure that schools do not receive less than they have in previous school-years. All of these components resulted in cautious optimism in 2020, but now advocates fear that the staggering amount of funds universal vouchers will be awarded will prevent the state from funding the FSFP. With both FSFP and universal vouchers in the state budget, it is becoming more difficult to reject one without impacting the other; however, with universal vouchers costing the state up to $1.13 billion during the first year (McClory, 2023, para. 1), it's hard to believe it won't impact the available funds for public education. So, it seems administrators have reason to be concerned. "Although direct cause and effect is difficult to prove, the bottom line is clear: As states transfer millions of dollars to private hands, there are fewer available state resources for projects that serve the public good, from mass transit to public parks, libraries, and schools" (Abrams, 2023, p. 16).

Now, we live in a time where we are used to schools often having to make deep cuts to keep up with flailing budgets, but how sustainable is this *really*? I previously mentioned that I was fortunate enough to attend a school district that provided us with College Prep, Advanced Placement, College Credit Plus, and career-technical education so we were able to explore future opportunities. This school district also provided athletics, music, art, and more. But what happens if one year they are forced to cut the Career-Technical Education? Followed the next year by music and art, and shortly thereafter College Credit Plus has to go? With these cuts begins the exodus of caring, talented teachers, and their leaving brings the end to Advanced Placement and College Prep. And very soon, the only thing that is left to cut are teachers' salaries and critical programming, including English as a Second Language, special education, and busing. Now imagine the school district we're talking about didn't start out with commodities such as Advanced Placement and College Credit Plus. What if the school district that is faced with severe cuts only offers critical and mandatory programming? How would that school district handle these cuts? How would this impact the administrators, teachers, and parents? More important, how would this impact the students?

Facing the Inevitable: Inside the Experience of an Administrator During the Privatization Movement

With the end of the 2032–2033 school year, Ms. Smith breathes a sigh of relief. It's been a tough decade since EdChoice was expanded, and Ohio moved to a universal voucher model. With this move, the state saw an immediate increase of $528 million in expenditures due to students who had already been attending private schools taking advantage of the program, and school districts saw an immediate loss of $68.5 million due to new students taking advantage of the program. Because of this, spending was tight, and districts had to make cuts in areas that weren't considered crucial, including extracurricular activities, supplies, and even busing.

Ms. Smith is the superintendent for District A, and she has felt the impact of universal vouchers more than most. District A's student enrollment is down nearly 50% since the program's expansion, but it hasn't been possible to cut the district's expenditures as quickly as they've lost state funding to the program.

Locking her office for the day, she can't stop the questions running through her mind: *Do they just expect me to stop paying our bills?* There is little left that she hasn't made cuts to, and what's left she knows is the difference between survival and ending up like some of the districts who had to close their doors in the next county over. Still, with the projected budget for the 2033–2034 school year, she knows she has to do something. Fortunately, the Board of Education agrees with her, and at their meeting earlier today they voted unanimously to hold a special election to pass an emergency levy. It won't solve all of the district's issues, but it will help for the upcoming school year, and since she has a good relationship with the community, she is confident it will pass. *At least this will buy us time to figure out a more long-term plan.*

I can't believe the levy didn't pass—do they not understand what is at stake? Ms. Smith's confidence had dwindled in the days leading up to the special election, as she did some last-minute canvassing.

"Why should I vote to raise my taxes to support a school district that my son doesn't attend?" asked one person.

"With all of the cuts you've already made, how do you still need more funds? Maybe you should take a pay cut!" shouted another.

Ms. Smith tried to explain, "You have to understand that School District A is important to our community. There are students who aren't able to attend Private School 1, Private School 2, or who wouldn't benefit from the Charter School. If we are able to get our funding back on track, we'll be able to reinstate some of the cut programs, and maybe even look at building new facilities."

Ms. Smith pleaded with everyone she spoke to, but she could tell they weren't convinced. With the failure of the levy, she's forced to make more cuts, including bringing an end to all extracurricular activities, English as a Second Language programming, and busing, a reduction in the budget for supplies, and what she had been trying to avoid at all costs, pay cuts.

The teachers and parents have to understand. There is a way out of this hole, but right now we have to make cuts where we can.

The 2033–2034 school year started without issue, it seemed as though the teachers and parents did understand, and the students were in high spirits. But then a month into the semester Mr. Eebs handed in his notice, followed by Ms. Amels, and finally Mr. Christle, all wonderful, popular teachers, but who could also no longer bear the stress of working in an under-funded school-district, while barely earning enough to live on. Around the same time, Ms. Smith noticed that absences and truancies were higher than she'd ever seen before, and student attitudes started to change. With the loss of teachers, classes were forced to combine, resulting in classrooms crammed with nearly 40 students, creating difficult learning conditions. By the end of the school year, the school district was receiving low rankings in all four report card measures, including achievement gap closing, progress, and graduation rate, and Ms. Smith's worst fears were answered when she was informed that they would be consolidating with another District.

District B isn't a bad district, but how are our students supposed to find a way to their school buildings when they've had difficulties making it here?

As the state pulls more funds out of our public schools, including District A, more responsibility is thrust on the administrators and every citizen of the district to agree on cuts and find a way to raise additional funds. To some, this may seem like an easy feat—but consider that we're talking about a district that barely has enough money to keep its doors open. Do you really believe that if the citizens of that community had the ability to better support their schools they wouldn't jump at the opportunity? The unfortunate truth is that the districts faced with these difficult situations are the districts that rely on state funding the most. They are the lower-income districts that don't have the property values, nor the income to raise the necessary funds to retain compassionate and innovative teachers, nor the funds that could also provide busing, College Prep, and extended learning opportunities to their students. Now, let's take another look at District A's situation, this time through the perspective of a parent and her two high-school aged children.

Facing the Inevitable: Inside the Experiences of a Parent and Her Children During the Privatization Movement

"I can't get my kids to District B every day," Miss Clark thinks to herself upon hearing the news that District A will be consolidating with them. *"I've always supported public schools, but we're going to have to look into some of the other options in the area."* Miss Clark has heard a lot of good things about Private School 1, so she reaches out to an admissions representative and initiates the application process for her two high school-aged children, Joe and Mary. As she sits there filling out the application, the admissions rep asks her some questions that make her feel uneasy, including questions about her ethnic background and financial situation. But it was one specific exchange that brought the conversation to a quick halt:

> "I notice you go by Miss Clark and not Mrs., did your husband pass away?"
>
> "No, I was never married."
>
> "Okay, Miss Clark, I think we have everything we need. We'll let you know shortly about whether or not we'll be able to admit your two children."

Feeling as though her kids didn't have a strong chance of being admitted to this school, she briefly looked into Private School 2, but realized that even with the full $15,000 per student the state was now offering in vouchers, she wouldn't be able to afford to send her kids there, unless she were to find a second job. Her last option was the Charter School. She had seen a flier about an admissions info-session that would be taking place this Saturday, but there's no way she'd be able to get off work that quickly to attend, so she decided to make an appointment to meet with an admissions representative the following Monday.

"Well, Miss Clark, your children are both qualified candidates for our school, but unfortunately, our info-session on Saturday was a requirement for admission for this fall."

"I didn't know it was a requirement, the flier didn't say that, and I wasn't able to take off work. Isn't there anything I can do—my kids need to be in school."

"Unfortunately, we pride ourselves on holding firmly to our policies, that's why our students do so well, so there's nothing I can do at this point. If you'd like, I can add your children's names to our waitlist, and if there are any last-minute openings that we need to fill I can let you know."

"Yes, please, I would really appreciate anything you can do to help me get my kids in your school for this fall."

Forced with the reality that her kids may have to attend Private School 2, Miss Clark starts looking for a second job to help cover the tuition. Fortunately, a few days before the start of the fall semester she heard from the Charter School, and her kids would be able to start there on day one. They have to walk, but at least it's school. Unfortunately, what Miss Clark didn't understand about this school is that it's a "no-excuses" institution. Tardiness is punished with detention, and her kids didn't realize quite how long the walk would take on the first day, so they start the semester off on the wrong foot. After serving detention, and making sure to leave plenty early for school from now on, things start to look as though they are going smoother.

But it's a hard adjustment for Joe and Mary Clark, as they were used to having a close relationship with other students and their teachers at District A, and at the Charter School they aren't allowed to speak unless they are called on. The Charter School also has a strict policy related to paying respect to teachers and guest speakers, which involves keeping your eyes up front, and following them if they move around. Mary had always been a daydreamer, and one day she let herself wander off into her own world. It wasn't long before she was asked to leave the room, and found herself in front of the principal as he phoned her mom.

"Hello, Miss Clark, this is Mr. Jax with the Charter School. I have Mary in my office, and I'm afraid there's a problem. I'll need you to come in for a chat," he says flatly.

"I'm so sorry for whatever issue there is Mr. Jax, but I'm at work, and I'm not able to leave," Miss Clark responds sincerely.

"Okay, thank you for your time," he says, immediately hanging up the phone.

When Miss Clark arrives home that evening, she is shocked to hear that both of her kids have been expelled from the Charter School. She works the late shift the next day, so she is able to stop in to the school to speak with Mr. Jax. She can hardly believe it when he doesn't even invite her into his office, and dryly says:

> "I'm sorry Miss Clark, but you were told from the beginning, we are very strict with our policies, and that's what makes our students successful. You missed the info-session over the summer, and we were flexible enough to still offer your children seats in our school. Your children were then late for school on the first day, but we gave them another chance. Daydreaming and not paying attention in class is unacceptable, and unfortunately, we don't have any more chances to extend to your children."

At that point, Mr. Jax walks back into his office and closes the door. Miss Clark sits for a moment, feeling perplexed and hopeless. When she found out her kids had been accepted to the Charter School, she had stopped looking for a second job, so she wouldn't be able to pay the tuition for Private School 2. After a few minutes she decided to drive to Private School 2 to see if there were any options for a payment plan. Her desperate feelings only increase when she meets with an admissions representative from Private School 2 and is told that her kids wouldn't be able to start there until the following Fall semester unless she is able to pay the full tuition. Unfortunately, because her kids had started the school year at the Charter School, the funds available to them through an EdChoice voucher were already distributed to the Charter School, and would not be released to Private School 2.

* * *

The previous narrative features a school district from 2033 having to close their doors because of the privatization movement, and the impact this can have on individual families.

What if I told you that this isn't a work of fiction, but something that has already impacted school districts and families across our nation? In the media we often hear praise about how private and charter schools have changed the lives of students, and produced impressive test scores, graduation rates, and college placement. It's important to understand that with no mandated reporting processes, the numbers that we see do not necessarily represent the whole picture. A school may report a 99% college placement rate, but that doesn't take into consideration the numerous students who were forced out of their school and/or never graduated. Additionally, even though there are some extremely successful charter and private schools, these small, elite institutions are not the ones that will be receiving a large portion of school vouchers, and their students are not the ones who were ever at-risk of experiencing the negative outcomes of vouchers on public education.

The Haves and the Have Nots

The detrimental impact of the privatization movement on public school districts at risk of closing their doors is merely one aspect of the problem. As illustrated in the preceding imaginary scenario, many families, despite a "school voucher" and their best efforts, would be unable to afford the tuition to send their children to a private school. In the media, we frequently hear about how private and charter schools have changed students' lives and delivered outstanding test scores, graduation rates, and college placement. However, it is just as critical to understand and report on the fact that, aside from the lack of any real mandated reporting processes to truly confirm what is actually happening these private schools, what is also not being discussed are the populations of students who will never benefit from the privatization of public education and will be "left behind" in public schools with depleted funds.

As a result of the huge uptake in voucher programs during the twenty-first century, many scholars have written about the negative impact of vouchers when students move to "subprime providers" utilizing school vouchers in private schools, where in a lot of cases the schools have been proven to deliver nothing but low academic performance, discrimination (not all can get in), etc. I (Carolyn) would like to focus the narrative on how the education movement's use of the voucher system to pay for private schools affects and undermines not only the public education system, but also the many student populations who have "no choice" but to rely on public education. I want to acknowledge up front that I am a proponent of parents having the option to choose the best school for their child, so this is not about removing that choice from parents but rather ensuring that the students who remain in the public school system continue to receive adequate funding, resources, and the ability to obtain a high-quality K–12 education as well.

> I remember it like it was yesterday. Waking up early in the very rural community that was a racially and economically segregated little town in Missouri, getting ready, and being excited to get to school. I understood

even then that we didn't have much, but I didn't care because I had school. I loved school and learning. I am pretty sure that passion came from Mrs. Alice Johnson, an educator in the school district who just also happened to be my very much older cousin (an elder in my family).

I remember going to her house when I was not in school to visit with her, where she always fed me well, but also had me read a lot on every visit. Mrs. Johnson would challenge my understanding of what I read, tell me wonderful stories about the children in her classroom, share with me all the adventures she had had and that I could someday have, and always spoke with me about the importance of getting an education. She was BIG on that—obtaining your education no matter your circumstances.

On each visit, she would be sure to tell me my way out would be getting an education, and by education, she meant not only getting through elementary, middle, and high school, but also obtaining a college education. This same cousin taught at the only elementary school that I remember in the district. I remember some Black students but mostly the White students who went to the school because, back then and even today, there was clear separation in the community between what one might call the "haves and have nots," and I lived then with the "have nots."

Universal Public Education

Early advocates of public education called for universal "public schools" that would be available to all children, free of charge, and funded by the state, as they truly believed this public school system would "benefit the whole nation economically" and was the means to "eliminate poverty, crime, and other social problems" (Kober & Rentner 2020, p. 3). Interestingly, these same advocates also truly believed that, "when children from diverse backgrounds interacted in the same classrooms, they would find common ground, learn to respect each other, and learn skills of getting along" (Kober & Rentner, 2020, p. 5). So universal public education became a reality, but as an African American female from humble beginnings, I learned at a young age how children of color were denied a free education or eventually attended underserved and unequal schools, even being forbidden to read. Even after federal laws were passed to make things better, I recall many of the stories that my family and community elders would tell about living with "Jim Crow laws" that kept school systems segregated and African Americans dealing with other exclusionary practices in their daily lives that persisted through the twentieth century.

Finally, after many decades, a Civil Rights Movement, federal legislation and judicial action (Brown vs. Board of Education outlawing state-sponsored segregated public schools), and court decisions, universal access to public education matured into the full pursuit of equal educational opportunity for all racial, ethnic, religious, and linguistic groups, as well as females and students with disabilities. Many schools began to extend their services to the community by offering breakfast and lunch programs to ensure students didn't go hungry, as well as after-school programs, safety, and other resources. Eventually, free public education became part of state constitutions, and according to Kober and Rentner (2020) by the second decade of the twenty-first century, public high school completion rates were a priority, with 90% of Americans aged 25 and older obtaining a high school degree in 2017.

Defunding Undermines Public Education and Communities

> By the time I was in high school, my family had moved to Ohio, where the schools were so different from the ones in rural Missouri where I grew up. There were lots more students, but still more White students at the time that I remember. The school was much larger, and being new to the city, I knew no one in the school. I was now in what I grew to understand was an urban school district, which I guess offered me even more opportunities but not as many as students in private school and would challenge me in many different ways.
>
> Again, I did really well in school and was an honor student, student leader, played in the band, etc., but my circumstances, from an economic standpoint, were not strong. I was what I now understand to be known as an inner-city, historically underrepresented, low socioeconomic student (and in college, I would have first-generation tacked on to my identity). It was in this urban school that I first encountered what are called "vouchers" (the official term may have been something else), but vouchers were not defined then in the same context as the voucher system is today, which removes public tax dollars from public schools to support enrollment in private or charter schools. My memory of vouchers is receiving them so I could purchase a coat or some clothes for school. I remember being teased because of what I wore or how I looked, but while it was not a good feeling, I didn't care as much because, again, all I cared about was getting that education that Cousin Alice had instilled in me to never give up on obtaining. I remember just being happy that I had a coat or clothes and really staying focused on doing well in school, as I knew this was the only way I'd get to college.

But all this talk of current day vouchers has made me think about what if there had been a voucher system back then where an inner city, economically challenged student like me could have a parent take money from the public school and move me into a "better" charter or private school? As I imagine this past alternate world, I wonder, and many questions come to mind.

How would my mother have known about it, or who would have made sure she was truly informed about the voucher system? If there had been this voucher system, who would have decided which students and parents were made aware of it? I wonder if my mother had known about it, given our economic status, would we even have been able to take advantage of this new voucher system? Who would have helped her pay the difference between using the voucher and the cost of going to a private or charter school?

How would I have gotten to the new school, which I am most certain would have been further away? The flip side is that I now wonder, if there was a voucher system and dollars were taken away from my district schools to go to private and charter schools, what resources would I have not had access to because the money that could have helped us obtain those goals would have been given to more privileged students and families? Needless to say, during my elementary and high school years, a voucher system was never a topic of conversation in my household, unless like I said, it was being used to help with clothing or other needs. I am pretty positive there would have never been a discussion about utilizing "vouchers" (or scholarships, as they now call them) or tax payer dollars to move me, as a smart "have not" from a public school, to a private or charter school with the "haves."

According to the Ohio Department of Education (2022A), during the 2021–2022 academic school year, the state of Ohio had a total of 1.6 million public school students. That year, 32.5% of those 1.6 million in Ohio were students of color, with Black/Non Hispanic (16.7%), Hispanic (7.0%), and Multiracial (5.9%) making up the largest percentages. Also, 46.6% of Ohio students were economically disadvantaged (households with incomes at or below 185% of federal poverty (Churchill 2023, p. 10) with 16.2% being students with disabilities. These numbers are important to know because according to Abrams and Koutsavlis (2023), over 24 states in the US have or are considering one or more voucher proposals that might erode access to well-funded, public K–12 education for these students despite the fact that these voucher programs will only serve a small percentage of the nation's children. Abrahms and Koutsavlis (2023) also point out that this is despite the fact that 90% of PK–12 students in the U.S. continue to attend public schools and the public school enrollment continues to increase (especially among high-need students).

But according to Hinh (2023) and others, "there is limited evidence of vouchers expanding opportunities for students with the highest needs" (p. 8). As many reports have called out, there is a low acceptance rate of the highest needs students (i.e., students of color, students with low socioeconomic status, students with disabilities, students in rural communities, etc.) into these private schools, even when voucher systems using public dollars are the funding source. So, this is then one of the major issues with the current proposed school choice voucher system because the most in need students are once again being left out. As a child, I would have had multiple high-need identities and would have been totally dependent on the local public school system to even have a fighting chance at a decent education and certainly one that will get me to college. But just like the other students and contrary to some beliefs, it would have not been about my ability and motivation because studies have proven that despite sometimes very challenging circumstances "black males and females have high educational and career aspirations" (Scott-Jones & Clark, 1996, p. 522).

There must be a better method or process of offering parents "choice" of where to send their children to school while ensuring that all students receive a "high-quality" education and adequately funded public education. Many in this country worked hard and lost their lives fighting against racial and social inequities. To uphold the legacy of what these movements stood for, we must provide access to high-quality education for all students to honor these movements and ensure no students are "left behind." The undermining of public education not only negatively impacts higher needs students, but can have a profoundly negative impact that is far reaching into school districts and communities. "School vouchers perpetuate existing disparities in our K–12 funding and tax systems to further racially and socioeconomically segregate our education system" (Hinh, 2023, p. 1). Public schools that are consistently underfunded face shortages of funding for textbooks and supplies, and have a hard time keeping up with fixed costs and building maintenance. This lack of funding for public schools also leads to "fewer available state resources for projects that serve the public good, from mass transit to public parks, and libraries" (Abrams & Koutsavlis, 2023, p. 16).

Benefits of Well-Funded Public Education

I agree with Kober and Rentner (2020) who stated the reason "public schools came into being—preparing people for jobs and citizenship, unifying a diverse population, and promoting equity, among others—remain relevant, even urgent" (p. 7). Public schools not only are at the heart of educating our nation, but many times serve as community centers and shelters in times of disasters or emergencies. There are problems with public schools, to be sure. But researchers have proven over and over again that

> Schools that were most able to enhance the academic achievement of low-income and minority youths had rigorous academic standards (Sizemore, 1988); actively involved parents (Chan, 1987; Epstein, 1984; Moles, 1982); and social services that were integrated into the organization and activity of the school (Comer, 1999). Communities were shown to foster resilience when they had high availability of social resources and opportunities for youths to participate in programs in which they received adult aid in completing academic tasks and developing new interests and skills (Benard, 1991; Nettles, 1991; Wang, Haertel, & Walberg, 1994). (O'Connor, 2002, p. 856)

The success of our nation depends on keeping our public schools highly-funded and providing equitable and equal access to a quality education for all students.

Navigating Voucher Programs as a Parent: School Choice in China

It is also important to recognize that the potential for these policies to lead to further underfunding of public education impacts not only educators and students, but also parents. The idea that individual school choice could be financed by public education funding was a new concept to me (Dongxia) when I came to the US from China. In China, parents, to an extent, pay for public education through the need for afterschool tutoring to supplement traditional schooling, and the high mortgages necessary to attend school in a high-ranking district. Through enrolling my child in public education here in the US and studying education as a PhD student, I am now learning first-hand how the underfunding of public education can negatively affect families. While my child has had a good experience in a public school in Ohio, I am starting to see the impact of funding cuts, which become more probable as voucher programs take money away from the public school system.

When my daughter started elementary school in China in 2017, I felt temporarily relieved because that meant we could take a break from thinking about school district residency while she was enrolled in the school. It took us almost two years to find a property in a school district with a relatively high reputation. If not taking "school" as the most critical factor in our house hunting, we would have had many other options, like a better location, or a larger space with much less burden of mortgage on our shoulders. But finding a public school with a good reputation, in a nice neighborhood, was our goal during those two years, and our footprint had covered virtually every single real estate compound in Southern Chengdu district. We did what Chinese parents usually do for their children, and ended up paying 25% more than our budget for the new home.

My daughter loved her school even though she had a lot of homework. There were 48 students in her class with one head teacher teaching Chinese language arts, and another two teachers teaching math and science. I dropped her off at her school at 8:15 every morning and was supposed to pick her back up at 4:30 in the afternoon. It was quite a challenge for me to do this because I was still at work, but I was able to enroll her in an after-school program. Like having a full-time job, she was pretty much worn out after the day, but she did not get to rest until finishing her homework. At the beginning of the 1st grade, she spent about one-hour writing and practicing the words she had already been familiar with. As the semester progressed, she had to spend 2–3 hours on homework every evening. Most of the time I sat with her to go over the lessons when she struggled with comprehension. I gradually realized that it was not a problem of her comprehension; rather, it was common for teachers to teach one thing and students to be tested on something different. All teachers followed the same guidelines and curriculum, but the actual teaching in the classroom varies, as does testing. As a result, parents must take on the responsibility of helping their children at home, or sending them to a training institution.

If there was no standardized testing for scores, I assume that most parents, myself included, would much rather support a happy childhood for our children. Unfortunately, most parents must help their children get through the tests since there is no alternative way for students to move up in the system. The education training industry has expanded since 2004, a marketing report revealed that K–12 test training will grow by approximately $70 billion by 2027 in China (Technavio, 2023). In a sense of a much more manageable number, the tutoring sessions I arranged for my daughter were approximately $30 per hour. We could only afford a couple of hours a week, but we neither doubted whether we should do it, nor questioned whether every family could afford it. It was quite a common phenomenon in China.

Instead of spending time teaching children at home, or taking them to training institutions, another common phenomenon among parents in Chinese education is enrolling children in private schools. Even though public education of grade 1 through 9 in China is free, parents are still willing to pay for private education out of their own pockets for many reasons.

Mostly, they want to ensure students have a better-quality education with stricter discipline and higher standards, but less parental involvement.

My best friend, after seeing me and other friends spend too much time tutoring our children who continued to struggle with their education, decided to enroll her daughter in a private preschool right after she was born. One reason behind her decision was that this private education corporation has the highest acceptance rate to the best domestic colleges in the entire province; the other reason was that students attending primary school within this educational corporation would have a better chance of winning the lottery than being admitted to the corporation's secondary school. Unlike owning a property in a school district to send their child/children to the private school, parents must: 1) help their student pass an interview; and 2) pay the tuition upfront.

During the interview for admission to elementary school, my friend's daughter was asked a lot of questions about Chinese language arts, English, and math, etc. Just like every other parent, she had her 5-year-old daughter sit in a training center for months to prepare for this interview. After being admitted, she received a bill of more than $16,000 for the first year's tuition, while the average income per person in Chengdu city was only $6,728 in 2021 (Liu, 2022).

Navigating Ohio Voucher Programs

I could never afford a private school like that, nor would I expect someone else to pay the private school tuition for us, so I didn't believe that students could go to private or charter schools with other people's money until learning about school vouchers in the United States. Stemming from my previous experience with school choice in my home country, my instinctive thought the first time I heard about school vouchers was that these must be a kind of benefit that comes along with American education. Because of this, my initial question was if I could take advantage of the vouchers to get my daughter into private education, just like my friend's daughter. Then I asked myself, "If every child went to private schools, why are there still public schools? What is the point of having different forms of schools in terms of public, private, charter, or homeschooling? Why would some other people pay for your child's private education?" The more I learned, the more questions I had surrounding school vouchers.

The first search result that comes up in Google for "voucher programs in Ohio" is "EdChoice Scholarship Program" on the official website of the Ohio Department of Education:

The Educational Choice Scholarship (EdChoice) Program provides students from designated public schools the opportunity to attend participating private schools. The program also provides low-income students who are entering kindergarten through 12th-grade scholarship opportunities. (Ohio Department of Education, 2023)

Both the EdChoice Scholarship Program and the Expansion Scholarship Program seem appealing to me, as they both claim to financially support students who want to attend private schools. The EdChoice Expansion Scholarship Program is particularly for students from low-income families. The families of students pay little or nothing as long as their income qualifies according to the Federal poverty guidelines. Through the scholarship program, students in grades K–8 will receive $5,500, and $7,500 for students in grades 9–12 (Hemminger, 2023, para. 9).

The Ohio legislature has supported voucher programs for nearly 30 years, but recently has worked to expand these. Senate Bill 11 and House Bill 11 (also as known as the Backpack Scholarship Program) expand the existing voucher programs, claiming that it would give parents the freedom to make school choices with financial support from the state (Honesty for Ohio Education, n.d.A; Honesty for Ohio Education, n.d.B). These bills emphasize the concept of "the money follows the student," meaning no matter where the student attends, money goes with them. Dating back to the 2021–2022 session in House Bill 290, the Ohio State House has expressed their intent to establish a school funding formula that allows families to choose the option for all computed funding amounts associated with students' education to follow them to the public and nonpublic schools they attend. State Rep. Marilyn John, one of the bill's sponsors, said that the bill would empower the parents and families who want the best education for their children to have options when it comes to making a choice (Tebben, 2023).

In early 2023, Governor Mike Dewine proposed to change the requirement for the eligibility of household income to qualify for voucher programs in Ohio from 250% above the poverty line to 400%. For a household of four people, the poverty line of $120,000/year will be the qualification line for the voucher programs (Hancock, 2023). Meanwhile, the Backpack Bill will give students who are eligible for the voucher programs access to an educational savings account, which offers funds for supplementing costs associated with private education, with limited restrictions. The scholarship programs that offer the educational savings account under the Backpack Bill will gradually replace EdChoice Scholarship Programs starting in 2024 (Sziagy, 2023).

These policies seem to advocate for children's education, offering financial aid to the families in need. Who would not be happy to receive the money to support their children's education? However, I quickly realized that to a family of four, which happens to be the size of mine, $120,000 a year is actually a lot of money, but it still qualifies that family for vouchers. According to Hancock (2023), the majority of families in Ohio would actually qualify under this (para. 9), and as a result, a larger amount of public education funding will start being transferred to charter schools or private schools. These schools are for-profit organizations, aren't necessarily involved in education for the common good, and often aren't held accountable in the same way public education is. In these schools, students can be expelled or pushed out easily under strict policies, such as zero-tolerance, *but the funding remains, even when the student doesn't.*

The strictness of Charter school policies has constantly reminded me over and over of the school my daughter attended in Chengdu, the long hours that she and I sat at her desk to get the homework done, the punishment she got from her headteacher for some small mistakes, and all the anxiety and stress we got from her test results. When we came to Ohio after second grade, my daughter began attending the public school district where we reside. As a result, her learning has become more autonomous, self-directed, and meaningful.

Our family is grateful for English as a Second Language programming that is offered in Ohio public school districts to ensure that all English learning students' encounter meaningful learning opportunities. Her teachers have made tremendous effort with care and love to help her transition into a totally different and new language-speaking setting. The friends she has made at school have supported and encouraged her to make progress on a daily basis. It can be quite challenging for a family living in a foreign country; however, my eight-year-old got through that hardship successfully and happily with all the teachers, friends, and staff members at her school. If she goes to a charter school or private school in the United States utilizing vouchers, what difference would it make? Would she be able to learn English with joy? Would she be treated differently due to her limited English skills? Would she even be kicked out for underperforming? Would she even get accepted in the first place?

Additionally, the school bus has been a blessing for our family, as we are able to rely on it to get my daughter to school safely every day. As a parent coming from another country, I assumed that parents must pay for the bus, so I was amazed when I learned that the school bus is a "free" service. Students are easily transported between home and school, which gives parents extra time to focus on work and other things, without worrying about their child's safety on the way to and from school. In addition to that, my daughter met her best friends on the school bus, and they enjoy the time they get to spend together there.

Unfortunately, the school bus plan has been changed for this coming fall of the 2023–2024 school year. The school district has announced that the school bus will only serve grade K–8 students, and students who live two miles or more from the school. That means high school students will no longer have school bus transportation, nor will those who live within a two miles radius. For students who are able to take the school bus, grades K–8 will ride together, adding an additional 30 minutes or more on the bus to incorporate all of the pick-ups and drop-offs. This announcement was not easily made because the Board of Education knew how many families and students would be impacted by it, but it could save money to keep the schools running. The district also has made reductions or cuts in other aspects. For example, the gifted services for students in grades 3–5 will be no longer available starting in the fall, and all staff members have agreed to a 1% raise for the 2022–2023 school year, and no raise for the 2023–24 school year. Additionally, more reductions and cuts are likely during the Three-Year Cost Saving Plan for the whole school district to survive.

No matter whether students take the school bus or their families have to figure out the transportation on their own, it is clear that the school bus is in fact not "free." It is paid for by public school funding. Public schools in Ohio have three major funding sources, including the federal government, the state of Ohio, and local support. Federal funds, and other non-tax funds, make up the lowest percentage of public school funding, followed by state funding, which is supposed to provide a baseline of funding to make sure students have adequate education, leaving the locality to make up the remaining funds. Local support has been the primary source for Ohio public education, which is primarily funded by local property taxes, the lottery, and/or other income taxes.

Our school district is considered as a wealthy district, which impacts the level of funding they receive from the state, averaging around $3,668 per student (Theroux, 2023). The average total cost per student is $13,941 according to the FY22 District Profile Report (Ohio Department of Education, 2022B). That leaves more than an $8,000 gap for the district to raise from local sources to meet the educational needs for our children. The district isn't even able to benefit from post-COVID inflation, as the property tax dollars residents pay are fixed based on a previously approved tax rate as established in House Bill 920. Even if a property value increases, the tax rate for that property is adjusted so that the amount of taxes paid does not increase (Stabile & Rock, 2021, p. 14). For the district to raise more funds, a levy must be placed on a ballot to increase the tax rate, and voters voted down a levy in November 2022, which would have been the first increase to property taxes since 2004 (Theroux, 2023). Our public school district has about 3,000 students that rely on them for education. Financial struggles are not only hurting the district, they are also hurting every student and family, as well as the community.

Even with these financial difficulties, the school district still must provide school bus transportation for students in grades K–8 that live in the school district but attend non-public schools. As previously mentioned, under the updated voucher program, students in grades K–8 will receive $5,500, and students in grades 9–12 will receive $7,500 to attend a school of their choice (these rates are actually higher in the final, approved state budget, see below). The state of Ohio currently only gives $3,668.46 per student to our School District, and when one student leaves for a charter or private school the district loses that full $3,668.46, which is often more than they can cut due to bills, salaries, and maintenance, and the taxpayers of Ohio pay an additional $2,000-$4,000 to cover the remaining value of the voucher. While our school district is struggling to pay salaries, and families have limited access to transportation, our school buses give the students who are not even going to our public school a free ride.

This is in no way a fair game to play.

* * *

The United States has prided itself on providing opportunity to all, stemming from the education that our founders believed would be a cornerstone to our nation. We often take for granted that what we have, as it was our ancestors who fought to establish our current model of public education, but it is imperative that we fight for our children, and our children's children, so that they have the same educational opportunities that we've experienced., and so that they are provided the same resources that we took advantage of. Not one supporter of public education would claim that we don't need to improve our schools, but it is unfathomable to think that the way to do this is by defunding them. Ohio has taken its largest step yet toward the privatization of our schools, with the passing of the 2024–2025 State Budget (HB 33).

Throughout this chapter we've discussed how the privatization movement can and is impacting educators, parents, and students, but at the time, we only had projections to work with. In the new State Budget, the realities are beyond sobering. In his July 2023 post, Phillis (2023A) reveals that

EdChoice voucher funding was increased in the 2024–2025 State Budget by 76.7%. That includes $8,407 for high school students and $6,165 for students in kindergarten through 8th grade per student per year, amounting to $826 million over the following two years (para. 1). That's $826 million that could be used to improve our public schools. The FY22 District Profile Report, released by the Ohio Department of Education, shows that 77% of school districts in Ohio didn't receive the amount of funding this program provides for high school students, and nearly one half of the districts didn't even receive the amount of funding provided for kindergarten through 8th grade students (Ohio Department of Education, 2022B). Additionally, just because the state of Ohio claims that every child will be eligible for a voucher, that doesn't mean that every child has the ability to use this option. As Staver (2023) points out, "Most of the state's eligible nonpublic schools are located in and around its cities, leaving large swathes of Appalachia and rural Ohio without alternatives (para. 2) ... Increased eligibility is not equivalent to increased access" (para. 7).

We are in no way saying that parents and students don't deserve choices when it comes to education. What we are saying is that our tax dollars are public funds, and should not be used for private enterprise. What we are saying is that all of our children deserve an equitable education and opportunity. What we are saying is that we need to do a better job of improving our public schools, holding all educational entities accountable, and following the money.

References

Abrams, S.E., & Koutsavlis, S.J. (2023). *The fiscal consequences of private school vouchers*. Education Law Center.

Akron Beacon Journal. (2015, 30 May). *Charter schools misspend millions of Ohio tax dollars as efforts to police them are privatized*. The Center for Popular Democracy. https://www.populardemocracy.org/news/charter-schools-misspend-millions-ohio-tax-dollars-efforts-police-them-are-privatized#:~:text=A%20Beacon%20Journal%20review%20of,type%20of%20taxpayer%2Dfunded%20agency.

Caggia, M. (n.d.). *Horace Mann on education and poverty* (1848). Caggia Social Studies. http://www.caggiasocialstudies.com/docs/AH104/Mann

Calderone, A.J. (2023, January 29). Future of school voucher system is questionable. *Tribune Chronicle*. https://www.tribtoday.com/opinion/guest-columnists/2023/01/future-of-school-voucher-system-is-questionable/

Churchill, A. (2021). An overview of Ohio's new school funding formula, and a look at whether it might stick. *Ohio Gadfly Daily*. https://

fordhaminstitute.org/ohio/commentary/overview-ohios-new-school-funding-formula-and-look-whether-it-might-stick.

Churchill, A. (n.d.). *Ohio Education by the Numbers 2023* (6th ed.). Thomas B. Fordham Institute.

Cowen, J. (2023, February 26). School vouchers: There is no upside. *Network for Public Education.* https://networkforpubliceducation.org/blog-content/josh-cowen-school-vouchers-there-is-no-upside/

Daly, L. (2022). *Re-contextualizing how I view public education: An expiration of the Ohio Coalition for Equity and Adequacy of School Funding.* Ohio University Libraries & Special Collections. https://sites.ohio.edu/library-archives-blog/2022/12/06/oceasf-exploration/

DeRolph v. Board of Education. (1997). 78 Ohio St. 3d 193.

Dyer, S., & Reedy, M. (2022). The promised education movement. *Columbus Bar Lawyers Quarterly,* 30–37.

Hancock, L. (2023, January 31) School vouchers expansion would qualify families of four earning $111,000 a year under Gov Mike DeWine proposal. *Cleveland.com.* https://www.cleveland.com/news/2023/01/school-vouchers-expansion-would-qualify-family-of-four-earning-111000-a-year-under-gov-mike-dewine-proposal.html

Hemminger, B. (2023). Mohawk admin hopes to educate public, politicians on vouchers. *The Daily Chief-Union.* http://www.dailychiefunion.com/featured/mohawk-admin-hopes-to-educate-public-politicians-on-vouchers

Hinh, I. (2023). *State policymakers should reject K–12 school voucher plans: Proposals would undermine public schools.* Center on Budget and Policy Priorities.

Honest for Ohio Education. (n.d.). House Bill 11. https://www.honestyforohioeducation.org/hb-11.html#:~:text=House%20Bill%2011%2C%20%22Backpack%20Scholarship,used%20for%20private%20school%20education

Honesty for Ohio Education. (n.d). Senate Bill 11. https://www.honestyforohioeducation.org/sb-11.html#:~:text=%E2%80%8BWhat%20does%20Senate%20Bill,at%20participating%20chartered%20nonpublic%20schools

Jefferson, T. (1786, August 13). *From Thomas Jefferson to George Wythe.* https://founders.archives.gov/documents/Jefferson/01-10-02-0162

Kober, N., & Rentner, D. S. (2020). *History and evolution of public education in the US.* Center on Education Policy at The George Washington University Graduate School of Education and Human Development. https://doi.org/10.1177/0002764292035003008

Liu, T. (2022, January 22). *2021 per person capital disposable income of Chengdu residents.* Chengdu Municipal Development and Reform Commission. http://cddrc.chengdu.gov.cn/cdfgw/fzggdt/2022-01/21/content_995a33dba98349fd848fd72316a16c24.shtml

McClory, E. (2023, March 14). Private school voucher expansion bills are in House and Senate; cost is for one year, and bill could affect busing. *Dayton Daily News.* https://www.daytondailynews.com/local/ohio

-school-backpack-bill-has-113-billion-price-tag-nonpartisan-group-says/K6VY2LA7U5DK5KPVPV7FLJLS3Q/

O'Connor, C. (2002). Black women beating the odds from one generation to the next: How the changing dynamics of constraint and opportunity affect the process of educational resilience. *American Educational Research Journal, 39*(4), 855–903. https://rb.gy/h61pd

Ohio Auditor of State. (2022). *Findings for recovery of $117 million-plus issued against defunct Electronic Classroom of Tomorrow.* https://ohioauditor.gov/news/pressreleases/Details/5965

Ohio Department of Education. (2023, May 3). *EdChoice scholarship program.* https://education.ohio.gov/Topics/Other-Resources/Scholarships/EdChoice-Scholarship-Program

Ohio Department of Education. (2022). *Enrollment by student demographics (state)–Ohio.* (2021–2022) [Data Set]. https://rb.gy/agqq8

Ohio Department of Education. (2022). *FY2022 district profile report* [Data set]. https://education.ohio.gov/Topics/Finance-and-Funding/School-Payment-Reports/District-Profile-Reports/FY2022-District-Profile-Report

Ohio Department of Education. (2021, November 24). *Overview of school funding.* https://education.ohio.gov/Topics/Finance-and-Funding/Overview-of-School-Funding

Phillis, W. L. (2023, July 10). *EdChoice voucher funding increased by 76.7% in the state budget (HB33).* Ohio Coalition for Equity & Adequacy. http://ohiocoalition.org/wp-content/uploads/2023/07/CC3564-7.10.23.pdf

Phillis, W.L. (2023, July 5). *Vouchers for ghost students in the publicly-funded private voucher schools will infest the universal voucher scene.* Ohio Coalition for Equity & Adequacy. http://ohiocoalition.org/wp-content/uploads/2023/07/CC3561-7.5.23.pdf

Scott-Jones, D., & Clark, M. L. (1986). The school experiences of Black girls: The interaction of gender, race, and socioeconomic status. *Phi Delta Kappan, 67*(7), 520–526. http://www.jstor.org/stable/20403145

Stabile, R.G., & Rock, M.A. (2021). *Ohio school finance blue book* (2022–2023 ed.). Powerhouse Press.

Staver, A. (2023, July 12). Every child will be eligible for a school voucher but many won't be able to use them. *The Columbus Dispatch.* https://www.dispatch.com/story/news/politics/2023/07/12/ohio-passed-universal-vouchers-now-it-eyes-private-school-capacity/70399450007/

Sweetland, S. R. (2014). An exploratory analysis of the equity of Ohio school funding. *Journal of Education Finance, 40*(1), 80–100.

Szilagy, S. (2023, March 20). *Lawmakers consider expansions to Ohio's private school voucher program.* NBC4 WCMH-TV. https://www.nbc4i.com/news/politics/lawmakers-consider-expansions-to-ohios-private-school-voucher-program/

Tebben, S. (2022, February 17). Ohio House considers Bill for students to use public school money on private schools. *Ohio Capital Journal.*

. https://ohiocapitaljournal.com/2022/02/17/ohio-house-considers-bill-for-students-to-use-public-school-money-for-private-schools/

Technavio. (2023, April). *China after-school tutoring market by application, end-user and channel–forecast and analysis 2023–2027*. Technavio. https://www.technavio.com/report/after-school-tutoring-market-in-china-industry-analysis

Theroux, E. (2023, January). *Ohio School funding model issues*. Talawanda.org. https://www.talawanda.org/media/superintendent/FundingLettertoCommunity%201-%20Dr-%20T.pdf

Thomas B. Fordham Institute. (2023). *Ohio education by the numbers 2023*, (6th ed.)

4

Is School Choice Our Hope?

An Imminent, Hidden Tragedy

Shawnieka E. Pope
Dormetria Robinson Thompson
Jing Tan

We use multiple approaches and discourses to talk here about the tragedy of school choice and the voucher system. This chapter highlights and centers the voice, experience, and perspective of the parent/guardian, teacher, and scholar. It is through our depictions of these characters' experiences that we consider and examine the false hope that the school voucher movement has been selling to the public to serve the proponents' agenda/purpose/interests. We appeal to the imminent hidden tragedy in education by sharing our stories to advocate for a more transparent and democratic public education for every scholar. We use the word "scholar"—rather than student—to emphasize the importance of lifelong learning.

The word *scholar* empowers and speaks to a full life, to a growth mindset, to excellence, and to the hope for a bright future. In this chapter, we navigate between fiction and nonfiction discourse. The following fictive section unpacks how a parent's school choice ends in tragedy.

I Want the Best Educational Option for my Child: A Parent's Narrative

My mother was a single parent raising two children. We escaped the typical narrative of single parenthood and poverty as our extended family stepped up as our village to absorb the gaps often created as a consequence of single parenthood. With only a high school diploma, my mother was offered employment at a major pharmaceutical company in our hometown. The financial resources gained with this employment not only handsomely addressed our basic needs, but this opportunity also created a pathway and access to the resources of the working middle class. This newfound access included options for school choice, which was not a necessary consideration during her K–12 public education.

The public education available to my mother and her siblings represented such high quality. The educators, parental, and community engagement were signature features of the public education experience. My mother and her six siblings attended public school in our hometown. Her mother, my grandmother, worked as a teacher's aide for the largest school district in the area and she along with my grandfather were major proponents of neighborhood public schools. My uncles, my mother, and my aunt experienced great connections with the educators who also lived in the neighborhood. The relationships established with educators created an extended family and the connection to the school building itself kept the neighborhood scholars returning for many years. The school was a vital pillar in the community. There was such pride attached to attending the neighborhood public school. Public education would begin to pivot from one of the greatest assets in the neighborhood to one of the greatest tragedies in the neighborhood.

As my brother and I became school-aged, the neighborhood schools that once served as the community cornerstone began to shift significantly. The neighborhood schools slowly lost their luster and no longer represented the vital link for scholars. My brother and I attended public school within this district for K–8 instruction. However, my assigned high school within this school system had been identified as a failing school. My mother made the decision to enroll me in a local parochial high school that was literally next door to our apartment complex.

I would attend this parochial school for my high school education. I never considered the possibility of any unintended consequence for attending this private school, until two weeks before my high school graduation. On this fateful day, I was wrapping up course exams and other assignments when I was summoned to the dean's office. I had never stepped one foot into our dean's office during my entire high school career. I was a high honor roll scholar, a member of the National Honor Society, captain of the varsity cheerleading team, and I maintained membership in many other organizations. Given my active engagement, there was never a reason for the dean to call me to his office.

I learned that day that my mother had been unable to keep up with tuition. I had an outstanding balance. Reflecting now, I can only imagine the heaviness of this secret burden on her. I can only imagine how this may have caused so many sleepless nights. I can only imagine how powerless my mother felt knowing this information would inevitably leak from her silence in such a profound way. That day I would learn about this secret that would alter the trajectory of my life. The dean informed me of my outstanding balance. He shared that the administration decided to allow my participation in the graduation ceremony, but I would not receive my diploma or my official transcript. Given my high achievement throughout high school, I applied to a prestigious Historically Black College and University (HBCU) and was granted conditional admission pending the receipt of my official transcript. At the end of this nightmare, I walked across the stage to a blank diploma and the crushing awareness that my conditional acceptance to the prestigious HBCU would be rescinded. This was all surreal, like a nightmare—a true tragedy...

I am most certain when my mother made the decision to enroll me in this private parochial school she believed she was acting in my best interests. I believe that my mother felt in her soul that in bypassing the failing public high school I was assigned to, she was positioning me to win academically! But her very decision to choose the private parochial school had severe, unintended educational consequences. My enrollment in the private parochial "choice" created a massive barrier to my engagement in postsecondary education. My mother would have never intentionally placed me in harm's way. She saw my academic prowess and she believed she was curating a space for me to flourish and transition to the natural next phase of my academic journey.

I believe this decision continues to haunt my mother. The decision to engage in school choice did not create a seamless pathway to access institutions of higher learning. I can only imagine how she navigated my graduation day and the following Fall when I should have been leaving for college. I can only imagine what it must have felt like to watch my heartbreak and disappointment as I sought employment rather than enrolling in college courses. I have always wondered if given the opportunity to go back in time, would my mother exercise "choice" over the local public school I was originally assigned to. If I am being completely honest, there are moments when I, too, wondered about the what ifs. I am a firm believer that God orchestrated my life's journey, so I don't linger too long considering what ifs.

I believe similarly to my own mother, parents, and guardians who attempt to navigate the information before them and choose a school setting that will not only educate their scholars, but a school setting that will nurture and develop their whole child. Camile Wilson (2005) discusses the importance of considering key factors. These factors include the positionality of Black women, and especially the enduring power structure of oppression, and agency. These very factors serve as informants that guide Black mothers as they navigate the fullness of school choice for their children. And this very choice sometimes leads to tragedy...

Tragedy Turns Green

Dollar signs diminish Black and Brown scholars' intrinsic value in poor communities. Community, historical, and racial trauma thicken the air, impeding fruitful breaths. How could we talk about historical racial disparity in the education system without discussing Black and Brown scholars living in under-resourced communities? Far too many scholars arrive at neighborhood schools engulfed in trauma and come into contact with administrators and educators who are knowingly and unknowingly ill-equipped to meet their needs. In our class this summer, one of my classmates focused our attention on the impact of zip codes, how they have the power to prescribe access to resources. These very zip codes offer essential information, but elected officials, investors, and funders of charter schools and school vouchers only see green and not the tragedy of scholars being robbed of quality education that not only supports their cultural capital but embraces its empowering properties. In their book chapter, Lubienski et al. (2023) explore the claims and strategies of voucher advocates stating:

> ...we conclude that advocacy around vouchers is much more a manifestation of a political/ideological agenda than of an empirically based effort to

remedy educational inequity noting how efforts by advocates to shift their own criteria for evaluating their preferred policy proposals represents a significant concern for the scholarly community, policymakers, and stakeholders. (pp. 128–129)

When one follows the dollar signs, the greed and disregard for quality education for all are hidden in plain sight. If providing choice is of the utmost importance, why wouldn't all options present comparable offerings? If parent choice is the goal, equal funding should support public education. The overwhelming financial support for charter schools/school vouchers and the active defunding of public education discounts this notion of "choice." What parent would choose a school with a constantly diminishing bottom line? What parent would choose dilapidated school buildings and dwindling resources? Really, there is no true choice! Sanders et al. (2018) compare corporate Chicago charter schools to peonage sharecropping. During Jim Crow, Black families were offered the possibility of land ownership. Sharecropping was a predatory system allowing Black tenants to use the land of White owners and in return, tenants would share crops. "In similar fashion, parents who are 'sold' on charters are often compelled by the argument that they will reap greater educational opportunities, such as admission to selective enrollment high schools and to college, with accelerated options for success in the workforce" (Sanders et al., 2018, pp. 43–44).

Charter schools and school vouchers rise up in the midst of trauma and tragedy as a potential savior to save Black and Brown families from failing neighborhood schools. Charter schools promise innovation, beautiful buildings, and top-tier education with all the bells and whistles. Parents see the silver lining in charter schools and they choose the new best thing over the shell of education available within their own communities. Sanders et al. (2018) state, "The story has all the bells and whistles of a Hollywood movie—a public school system made up of mostly poor and minoritized students suffering from years of academic failure . . . In the end, the kids are saved by a knight in shining white armor" (Sanders, 2018, p. 2). Charter schools exploit both the pain and hope of Black and Brown parents who only want the best for their children. That burning hope veils their ability to critically examine how policies and procedures at their chosen charter school may harm their children. That burning hope neutralizes the impact of zero-tolerance practices their children must navigate unknowingly. And when their scholar clashes with these practices, the promise of hope disappears like an elusive nightmare. Black and Brown scholars are dismissed from this choice and the tragedy remains; those scholars return to defunded neighborhood schools.

Under-resourced schools available to Black and Brown scholars remain the tragedy. Access to sufficient education in a system fueled by greed and capitalism remains the tragedy. Wealthy investors and funders who are not educators, yet push their agendas and the illusion of choice remains the tragedy. School vouchers disguised as school choice are nothing more than a pipe dream sold to communities that were never intended to benefit from the educational system, . . . and that too, is the tragedy. According to White (2018), "It is important to weigh the promises of charter schools against their outcomes and their impacts on every child" (p. 71).

Like parents, teachers, too, have experienced the tragedies of school vouchers, especially when schools funded by them are not being operated with full transparency, proper management, and fiscal prowess. We will now focus on the experience of a teacher who taught at several public schools and private schools.

The Intersection of Hope and Tragedy: A Teacher's Unexpected Nightmare

It was the 2016–2017 school year and I was a Title 1 teacher at a public charter school in an urban city. This was my third-year teaching at the elementary school that served predominantly Black scholars. Without a doubt, the public school district in our city was underperforming for the most part. The first couple of years at my new school were great and I did not expect anything less during my third year.

My current superintendent was a fellow teacher at another charter school in the city. We worked together on the same team for three years and had loads of fun teaching and became more like family. She decided to start a charter school to continue the legacy of her parents who were both longtime educators. As she talked about her idea of starting a school, it sounded like a great opportunity. Our current place of employment was having some challenges with the school board as well as questionable activities with our superintendent. I felt like it was time to move on, so I decided to begin this new journey of working at a brand new, public charter school with my co-worker, and soon to be new superintendent.

Halfway through the 2016–2017 school year, my teaching career and life would take a turn that I could never have imagined!! My husband served on the school board at my charter school. He was recruited by my friend to a new position at the school and focused on parent engagement, based on his amazing engagement as a parent and the fact that his children attended another charter school for a few years in our city. One day he came home from work and began to tell me that the school's treasurer reached out to members of the school board regarding fiscal transactions that our superintendent had made. At the same time our state department of education was beginning to question components of the school's operation. Over and over again the past year or so, he would complain to me that the board did not know what she was doing and if they questioned her actions she made it seem like they were attacking her and not supporting her vision for the school. The school board attempted to keep her accountable, but she wanted to do things her way. Her view was that she was the victim of a tragic misunderstanding. Folks began to murmur...things began to stir...the nightmare was unfolding.

The allegations included items purchased yet receipts were missing, items purchased with school funds yet those items not present at the school but at her home, and travel expenses paid with school funds that were not connected to school activities. These are all bad allegations and I could not believe I was in the middle of this. It was surreal.

As emergency meetings began to occur and the school board voted for her to get leave with pay until the allegations could be verified, I went from feeling like my job was great and my co-workers were part of my family to hating coming to work and feeling like I was on an island all alone. My co-workers were no longer as friendly, especially when I mentioned to them that this was eerily similar to allegations from our previous charter school where many of us all taught together before working at our current charter school. I was married to one of the people who voted for her to be relieved of her duties and a fellow teacher with an administrative license became our interim superintendent. As news crews appeared at the emergency meetings, I was concerned for my husband. Would people in the community think he did not do his job? Would the state somehow come after the school board and charge them with being reckless? Would I somehow be involved in this investigation because of my husband's position at the school? Am I dreaming and when I awake will all of this be over? My mind was saturated with these questions with each passing day of this tragic, education nightmare.

State investigators eventually got a search warrant for the superintendent's home at the beginning of 2017. I will never forget looking on the news and seeing detectives and other law enforcement carry out various items. One large item that was purchased with school funds was found in her backyard. What in the world is going on? Can the nightmare stop?

The state auditor charged the superintendent and the former school treasurer of misspending thousands of taxpayer dollars. The state auditor said she made hundreds of debit card transactions. The school's treasurer signed checks to the superintendent for reimbursement for trips to conferences and per diem although proper documentation could not be found. Because they signed off on the check, the treasurer was held liable for his actions. The school's treasurer also negligently paid a late fee to the local electric company, which you cannot do with taxpayer funds in our state. Lastly, the treasurer incorrectly paid sales tax to vendors although the school is tax-exempt. His firm had to pay the money back as a result of the investigation. The superintendent was indicted in 2020. I am unaware at this time of the result of the case. The school board members were not found to be at fault in any way.

But the long horror continued. The school year ended very, very awkwardly—the superintendent was gone, my former co-worker became the interim superintendent, most of the staff and many of the families believed the superintendent was innocent, there was deep uncertainty about the upcoming school year, the Black-owned food vendor was unable to get their high-end, industrial catering equipment out of the building, and me feeling odd. Can I wake up now?

Due to the school closing, all teachers received unemployment. For the first time in my life, I was getting a portion of my hard earned check due to the allegations against the superintendent. Due to these allegations, I had to report my job searches and complete many official documents on a regular basis. Due to these allegations, I was back on the job market. Due to these allegations, Black and Brown scholars and families were dispersed once again, scrambling to find a new school for the upcoming school year. These families came to us after being dissatisfied with the local public school or other public charter schools. Yet, they find themselves scrambling for their next beacon of hope again.

We cannot get the 2016–2017 school year back. Yet, what can be learned from this tragedy? While I awoke from my charter school nightmare, it is a bad dream that should not have occurred. Whether the allegations were true or not is not my point. The tragedy is that me and a plethora of others were entangled in this tumultuous situation at all! No scholar came to school expecting to be misplaced by the end of the school year. Scholars came to school to learn. No teacher wants or deserves to experience sudden job loss. Teachers came to work to make positive impacts on the lives of their scholars. I cannot recoup the loss of my partial paycheck. Nor was I expecting to be a part of the statistics that state that there is a much higher teacher turnover rate at public charter schools compared to public schools (Naslund et al. 2019). No family enrolled their scholar expecting to have to go back on the school hunt by the end of the school year. Families enrolled their scholars to experience something different—a positive, safe space where learning would be innovative and equitable. No small business vendor hires staff and purchases industrial cooking equipment expecting a major revenue loss. The Black-owned catering company was relatively new and wanted to make sure our scholars received high-quality meals. No taxpayer files and pays taxes yearly expecting their hard-earned money to be in the middle of a horrific misappropriation of funds scandal. Thousands of tax dollars were spent on the establishment and operation of this public charter school. We were all a part of an educational tragedy that we did not deserve or ask for.

Call and Mission

Teachers do not become teachers for fortune. Teachers do not become teachers for fame. Teachers become teachers to make a positive impact on those they are blessed to take down the adventurous, rewarding, intense, and empowering road of education. And most teachers are tied to this awareness of calling.

This sense of call and mission, of making the lives of scholars better applies to public, charter, and private school teachers. For some teachers they see themselves fitting into the traditional cookie-cutter example of answering the question of "what do you want to be when you grow up?" and they reply, "a teacher." It is something they have always felt a yearning to do and they take the traditional route of going to school and graduating with an education degree and go on and teach in a variety of school settings including public, private, and charter schools. Additionally, I know many young and veteran credentialed teachers who have vacillated between all of these various school settings within their years of teaching. They are traditional cookies.

For others, like me, teaching was not our first profession, yet we too felt this eventual nudge, this call, to teach in a school setting. Many who become teachers as a second or possibly third career path go back to school and get an education degree. Meanwhile, others become teachers with a wealth of transferable skills, experiences, and non-educational degrees and a burning desire of hope to inspire, empower, and educate scholars. While we may not fit in this traditional cookie mold, we, too, are cookies. We are nontraditional cookies who also feel this sense of call and mission.

Charter schools in America are by and large able to forgo the traditional labor bureaucracy which consumes public schools (Naslund et al., 2019). Due to public school red tape, public charter schools and private schools are the beneficiaries of many cookies—those with teaching and non-teaching degrees. Public charter schools can set their own employment policies including compensation, hiring, and termination without infringing upon federal or state laws. For instance, I know of a phenomenal young non-certified Black male who has taught all school year in an upper elementary classroom at a public school with a long-term substitute teaching license. His classes' content area test scores were the second highest in the entire building this past school year. He has an excellent rapport with his scholars, is in school pursuing his teaching degree, and wants to return to the same school teaching the same grade and content area next school year with regular teacher pay versus being paid as a long-term substitute. He is an amazing teaching cookie. There are no other Black teachers in this public school that serves predominantly Black scholars. Is this what equity looks like?

The other important piece that needs to be noted here is that this grade and content area in this public school building has experienced certified teacher turnover for more than the past four years! No longer willing to wait on the public school district to do the out-of-the-box and equitable thing, he applied for a teaching position at a local public charter school. He has completed two rounds of interviews and was recently offered a contract as a classroom teacher at a public charter school. He was wrestling with a decision—he really wanted to stay at the public school where he has taught, but they did not offer him a teaching contract, so he accepted the teaching contract at the public charter school. Can you blame him? The Black and Brown scholars at the public school where he taught last year will lose yet again. A local urban school district will lose an innovative, passionate Black male (uncertified) teacher to the local public charter school that is willing to work with him as he completes his undergraduate degree. This is tragic.

Should *all* teachers go back to school if need be and get fully credentialed as teachers? My answer would be, "yes," of course. Should teachers or cookies of various experiences be viewed as the problem of school vouchers? I would say, "No." Teachers like me and others are absolutely victims of bigger systematic strongholds. The school voucher versus public school debate is larger than teachers. We are cookies called to teach the generations behind us. Who knows, maybe some of our scholars will grow up, take our place as teaching cookies, and advocate for better schools for all scholars, too.

Each present and future teacher's real-world experiences and positionalities vary. We bring ourselves to the field of education and into the hearts of thousands of scholars through varying lenses. Why are teachers and other highly female populated professions the lowest-paid professions? Why are classroom teachers predominately White females, yet most public school administrators and superintendents are predominately White males? Why do so many White teachers feel the need to "save" Black, Indigenous People of Color (BIPOC) urban scholars? How is it that with union support, ineffective certified teachers are able to move from building to building within a public school district, traumatizing scholars, yet a non-certified teacher with excellent test score results and great rapport with scholars is not able to get a teaching contract? There is much social justice work to be done within the field of education. The tragedies abound.

I became a teacher to inspire, empower, uplift, and expose my scholars to amazing academic, civic, and social-emotional opportunities—no matter the geographical location of the school. It was a call to duty and I was ready to report for the mission at hand. I became a teacher to give scholars the opportunity to experience the joys of learning and helping them to find their voice and vision for their tomorrows in spite of their zip code. I became a teacher not from a deficit model perspective, but from an asset model based on my own public school education. And at no time before 2016–2017 did I think teaching would lead me to experiencing the tribulations of teaching at a public charter school. The cycle of injustice for our scholars, families, and teachers continues. The call to duty and mission continues in urban, rural, and suburban schools: We must do better to ensure our teachers are not collateral damage amid the school voucher debate, beyond zip codes.

A Call for Equity in Schools in America: Beyond Zip Codes

In our PhD Plan assignment in Dr. Poetter's EDL 761 class, an introductory class to doctoral studies, I (Dormetria) began my paper with the following line:

> I am pursuing my PhD in Educational Leadership at Miami University because it is my desire to gain additional knowledge and skills that will enable me to be a conduit that will catapult a re-evaluation of our public school system in America.

From the very beginning of my PhD journey, I felt the nudge to do my part in making public education in America better than its current state. The divine orchestration of being in this class is an important piece of my nudge for radical social justice within public schools.

My parents sacrificed buying their first home so that my sibling and I would have an excellent public school education. My location, my zip code, allowed me to attend one of the best public school districts (both then and now) in the nation. The Niche 2021 Best Schools rated my home public school district at #848 out of 10,760 school districts in America. Many of my parents' friends were buying houses in other areas due to the opportunity of buying a nicer home at a more reasonable price. However, these same families were sending their children to private schools because while the housing market was better, the public schools were not the best. Why should families have to choose to buy a home or send their children to a private school because of the tension between zip codes and higher-quality schools? This is not equity. This, too, is a tragic nightmare.

I recall school being fun, loving to learn, and not being concerned with standardized tests. Testing dominates our current culture and climate in schools, and especially schools in urban centers spend more time on preparing to pass a test than they do on teachers and scholars being able to enjoy the adventures of learning! This is a very sad state of affairs for today's educators and scholars in far too many public and charter schools.

Additionally, I recall being introduced to Ghana by my White second-grade teacher and eating fufu as a class, and going on field trips to an array of places including museums and historic sites. I had classmates whose parents were congressmen, in the military, and working professionals. At the same time, there were students throughout my schooling who lived in low-income housing. Even in the suburbs, there are those who live in lower socio-economic status homes—and many people simply choose to ignore or judge them. Unfortunately, even within the same public school system, many school buildings serve both the "haves" and "have-nots." Positionality matters. Zip code matters.

While I did have some great teachers and experiences, this is not to say that my public school journey did not have some challenges! Unfortunately, a few times this has meant challenging the narrative of White teachers whose version of "history" was narrow, incomplete, or inaccurate as they shared their White colonized version of events. I had no Black teachers until I went away to college. Advocating for myself and others has always been in my DNA, and attending a public school in the suburbs did not afford me the opportunity to forget my Blackness among Whiteness. There were a few times that my parents had to step in due to the actions (or inactions) of teachers or administrators while my sibling and I attended school. For instance, my parents were active in my sibling's high school Black Parent Association (BPA). The school administration wanted to abolish the long-standing Black History Month event and have a multicultural event instead. Thanks to the advocacy of BPA, the Black History Month event continued. Amid White supremacy and erasure tactics, BPA and the Black students were able to acknowledge and celebrate our rich legacy and history on *our* terms.

Between all of the amazing opportunities my zip code and parents provided for me and my public schooling, I have seen education and actually the world, as mine—as long as I put God first, remember the sacrifices and contributions of my ancestors, work hard (which unfortunately means "work twice as hard" because of racism, according to my mom), and give back. From public schooling to life as an undergraduate, to my journey through two graduate programs, I have approached each step along my educational journey as moments of yearning to learn more by expanding my worldview. I see learning as a fun adventure, although it can be challenging at times. I believe with the right public school opportunities, along with family and community support, this can and should be the potential perspective of all scholars—no matter their zip code. It is my passionate belief that our current educational systems are not created or operated equally. The New Jim Crow of Schooling is alive and well. I believe that every child should have similar amazing high-quality public school experiences that I was afforded. A family's zip code should not determine if this is the case. The divide between the "haves" and "have nots" within communities and educational spaces in America is intentional. The educational system is successful in accomplishing the intended goal—deepening the learning and experiential gap of millions of scholars in schools based on zip codes.

This desire for more, to experience a beacon of hope amid a public school system that is not academically strong or a public school system that prioritizes certain school buildings with added resources over other schools in the same public school district is what thrusts so many students and their families into the world of public charter schools. Many families say to themselves, "What do I have to lose?" While the public charter school movement is supported more widely by Republican voters over Democratic voters, this gap has closed as families of various socio-economic dispositions and racial backgrounds are willing to take the chance of their scholars attending public charter schools that seem to have more opportunities for academic and non-academic success (Kitzmiller, 2020). The tension between zip codes and potentially better outcomes drives them to something different. Can you blame them? We all want what is best for our children, and our family. Each time money is taken away from public schools and given to public charter schools our local public school district loses. They lose funds, scholar talent, family buy-in, and the power of public school education.

The end result is that our most precious treasured gifts, our scholars, are thrown into the rushing, tragic current of school vouchers. They have no life jacket or oar as they tread through their educational journey with the support of parents or guardians who want the best for their scholars. They are simply hoping for something different and better. Unfortunately, far too many scholars feel as if they are drowning once they enroll at a public charter school. Below is one scholar's story.

Progressive Lens: A Scholar's Story

This part of the chapter uses the progressive stage of the currere process to "imagine a future" for scholars, which allows "usually buried visions of what is not yet present to manifest" (Pinar, 1994, p. 25). The following story engages in a fictional telling to imagine a future in the next three to five years from the perspective of scholars to illustrate how school vouchers turn into a tragedy for scholars, teachers, parents, and education itself. We hope that this progression never happens and that education will be a wonderful journey for every scholar.

* * *

I am a scholar in a midwest public school district. I go to school every day because that's what we are supposed to do. I live in a decent neighborhood with my parents. My home public school isn't bad because there is a teacher who cares about my learning, and I have made a few friends. As a scholar, I have heard from the adults around me about my school options. There are public schools, private schools, and homeschooling. Both of my parents have full-time jobs, so homeschooling has never been an option. I have always attended public schools because they were not bad around my neighborhood and private schools are too expensive for us as a typical, middle-class family.

Until one day, I heard about school vouchers from my counselor because I am an outstanding student at my school. My counselor asked me if I want to go to a private charter school for gifted children. He said that I am smart, and this charter school would be a better place for me to learn. And it's going to be nearly free because of an educational policy called school vouchers. I was surprised to learn this information from my counselor because I have never heard it before from my parents or from my teachers. I loved the idea of going to a more challenging school and having a better future. I went back home and told my parents about the school voucher program. They were shocked, too, when they heard that I could go to a better school without paying extra money. So, I applied for the private charter school for smart and rich kids, and passed their exams. I was really excited to join the school.

I loved everything I saw the first time when I walked into the charter school. It had a big library, and each student had their own school ID cards.

It was all worth it in the beginning even though my parents had to drive me to the school every day. The classes were challenging. We had to read 30 books a year. I liked reading, but not so much after that. I was good at math, but not so much after we had very difficult math problems to solve all the time. I liked school, but not so much after I went to this charter school. I was always doing my homework and didn't even have time to do anything fun. I gradually lost my smile and wasn't happy for a long time. Eventually, I was stressed out and had to see counselors.

My parents talked with the school and complained about the curriculum and instructional methods. The school did not care and said they didn't follow the state standards because they are a private charter school. They said I can go back to my home public school if I didn't like the way they work. But my home public school was closed because they lost their students and funding due to the school voucher program. All the teachers, even the one that cared about students, were fired because of the public school closure. Even if I wanted to go back to my home public school, *I don't have the choice anymore.* I could go to a public charter school, though. But our local public charter school is a dropout prevention recovery school and I know it's not the right place for me. I heard that one of the private charter schools near us closed in the middle of the school year because the enrollment didn't reach the business owners' expectations and the students have nowhere else to go but the public charter school. Our private charter school had total authority over how they worked and made all the school policies they wanted to, such as the students having to pay hundreds of dollars if they didn't pass some of the school tests. My parents were mad because the school didn't listen or do anything they said about my mental health. All I remember after that conversation was a lot of work, a lot of punishment, and a lot of helpless, hopeless moments. This was a tragedy while I was simply trying to survive my high school years.

I barely made it out because the teachers at the private charter school did not care about me. It was a nightmare. Later I learned that they have never done any professional training and none of the teachers were properly trained or licensed. The school only cared about its reputation, graduation rate, and test results. They didn't care about scholars' individual development as people. I got a very high score on my SAT, so the school was happy. But I was *not!* All I wanted was to get out of my hometown and start somewhere new. It took me a long time to recover after I got into college. I made friends and met professors who cared about me. I was smiling and felt happy again.

I wish I would have known what charter schools were. I wish my home public school had the same educational resources as the private charter school. I wish my parents would have known better about the school voucher program and the private charter school. I wish my counselor would have told me a little bit more about the pros and cons of applying for school vouchers. Now, when I think about my educational experience, I realized that the school voucher program is an intentional program to attack the public school system under the mask of school choice. I thought I took advantage of the school voucher program, but the truth was that the business runners of the school took advantage of me. They were not trying to make things better for us and I was fooled by the good narratives and public facing intentions of the program.

As a scholar, I urge my parents, my teachers, and my counselor to be more responsible and critical when it comes to school policy and to get a complete picture of the choices before they propose them to children. As a scholar, I advocate for a more practical education focused on critical thinking so that we are prepared to analyze a choice holistically and are able to make an educational decision as a responsible person. As a scholar, I want a quality education and educators who care about us, not the money.

* * *

I (Jing Tan) wrote the fictional story above to show how school vouchers can be a tragedy for scholars, teachers, and parents without supervision and transparency. Under the mask of school choice, vouchers often benefit only the people in power, not the scholars who need help. Privateers do not want to serve the marginalized scholars at schools and cannot hide their purpose of moving public school funding into private education. We need to expose their real agenda to the public so that we can prevent more tragedies from happening in education.

Synthetical Lens—Educational Tragedy

At last, we want to bring all our stories and tragedies together to synthesize, which means reconstructing and reconceptualizing the meaning of our work the present (Pinar, 1994, pp. 26–27). What is tragedy in education? It is when a good intention/narrative/policy turns into a nightmare for parents, teachers, scholars, and the community because the people in power want more money for themselves and do not care about education for the public at all.

Tragedy #1: For-profit corporate charter schools "forced students to pay fines of approximately $200,000 per year for minor infractions, such as not wearing belts," and required students to repeat an entire school year for failing a single class, unless they transferred back to their neighborhood schools, so that the schools can fool the public by hiding the dropout rate and advertising their high graduation rate and college acceptance rate (Sanders et al., 2018, p. xi).

Tragedy #2: Orleans Parish School Board (OPSB) fired 7,500 school employees, who were mostly African Americans with livable-wage jobs and had been on Hurricane Katrina disaster leave without pay, including teachers, administrators, support personnel, bus drivers, etc.—all let go illegally contrary to local and state policy (Sanders et al., 2018, p. 15).

Tragedy #3: Scholars were denied enrollment into charter schools because of their disability and students with special needs were ignored, punished, even bullied once they were admitted into charter/private schools (Sanders et al., 2018, p. 23).

Tragedy #4: Teachers answer the call to duty to educate scholars in public charter schools only to experience the consequences of improperly functioning schools.

Tragedy #5: Scholars and families have to find a new school once their public charter school closes.

Tragedy #6: Far too many Black Indigenous People of Color (BIPOC) scholars and families take advantage of private school vouchers only to be forced to withdraw due to not being able to pay for the balance of private school tuition.

As educators, we worry about scholars who know about school vouchers, but don't really know what private schools and other charter schools can really do to them without supervision and transparency. We worry for parents and guardians who want the best for their kids, but are fooled/lied to by the political narratives that are presented with seemingly good intentions. We worry for teachers because they don't have enough power to protect their teaching career if schools and people in power can fire them anytime for their own agenda. We worry about the future generations' education because of the overemphasizing of STEM education and the lack of critical thinking in school curriculum.

For scholars, how do we assess their learning and success at schools? It's a tragedy that school voucher programs predominantly focus on test scores, graduation rates, and college attendance in order to sell the programs

(Lubienski et al., 2023, p. 137). These alternative options also have "deficits in other areas that arrest [scholars'] critical thinking skills" (Sanders et al., 2018, p. xi). For example, Sanders et al. (2018) mentioned that "Charters are notorious for their emphasis on tested subject areas—mainly reading and math. The loss of social studies—civics and history—has led to a significant decrease in critical thinking and problem solving" (p. xii). Scholars are different from each other and learn in different ways. Labeling a scholar or a school based on the test scores and education standardization have to be reassessed and replaced by a better evaluation system that empowers scholars' differences.

School vouchers and charter schools have some good intentions in them. That's why the public can be fooled by their narratives. If they can really provide quality options for scholars who don't have access to the education they want, school vouchers could be great with clear purposes and agendas. But the reality is that they have been serving as political tools to transfer public education funding into private schools, where the privileged scholars already have a lot more educational resources compared with public schools, such as field trips, libraries, and sports fields/equipment. That's a tragedy! When you have good intentions and narratives, but the reality is a mess and hurts the scholars whom the programs were supposed to help, the end result is tragedy.

For parents or future parents, we know that there is a universal decision we have to make: Where would I want my children to go to school? It is an important decision to make for a parent, one that will have a lasting impact on our precious scholars. The reality is that if you prefer public schools, you very often have to live in a nice (which means expensive) neighborhood. If you prefer private schools, you might worry if your children will be treated fairly if the scholar population in private schools is made up of rich and privileged families. What makes a private school private? It's not only their expensive tuition, but also the autonomy to hire any teachers and implement any discipline or punishment policies they care to. They make the rules, and they don't have to follow the state guidelines or share them with the public.

Our purpose for this chapter is not to indict all charter schools or suggest the ill-intention of every charter school in America. Our hope in this discourse is to enlighten and call to action the critical examination of the tragic condition of public education and the impact of the privatization movement on them. Afterall, public education is an essential component of a democratic society. There are many layers and perspectives to consider. We are hopeful that by viewing this public crisis through the lens of the parent/guardian, teacher, and scholar you can make a human connection to the tragic consequences that are both real and possible.

References

Kitzmiller, E. M. (2020). "We are the forgotten of the forgottens": The effects of charter school reform on public school teachers. *Harvard Educational Review, 90*(3), 371–396.

Lubienski, C., Brewer, J. T., & Malin, J. R. (2023). Bait and switch: How voucher advocates shift policy objectives. In K. Welner, G. Orfield, & L. A. Huuerta (Eds.), *The school voucher illusion: Exposing the pretense of equity* (pp. 124–147). Teachers College Press.

Naslund, K., & Ponomariov, B. (2019). Do charter schools alleviate the negative effect of teacher turnover?. *Management in Education, 33*(1), 11–20.

Pinar, W. F. (1994). *Autobiography, politics, and sexuality: Essays in curriculum theory 1972–1992*. Peter Lang Publishing.

Sanders, R., Stovall, D., & White, T. (2018). *Twenty-first-century Jim Crow schools: The impact of charters on public education*. Beacon Press.

Wilson, C. (2005). School choice and the standpoint of African American mothers: Considering the power of positionality. *The Journal of Negro Education, 74*(2), 174–189.

5

The Voucher Movement is Personal

Knowledge to Action and Manifesting (Re)Action

Cerelia V. Bizzell
Elizabeth Rae Kerr
Jacqlyn Schott

In this closing chapter, we take a currere approach in order to synthesize the ideas presented in the book and extend the conversation by sharing ways to get involved in fighting the privatization of education and supporting public education. The chapter centers around three characters—a teacher, a parent, and a higher education practitioner. The characters gather in a fictional setting—a town hall regarding the closure of James Elliot High—to advocate for public education, while also reflecting on their own relationships with the school choice movement. All three characters are connected by their desire to stop being complacent and start advocating for public schools. The chapter concludes with a Call to Action, a declaration of these characters' desires to see public education fully supported. Ultimately, the Call to Action belongs to this book's authors.

The authors of this chapter chose to reimagine our own perspectives through hypothetical characters that connected to us in personal ways. Some aspects of the characters are representative of the authors, while other aspects are imagined in order to capture the voices and perspectives within the previous chapters. Our characters consider their connections to school choice, and the charter and voucher movements. Adhering to the currere approach, our characters incorporate both our personal and professional lives (Pinar, 1994) in order to demonstrate how school choice is not an isolated phenomenon, but rather has implications throughout one's existence and in the world at large...

Each character's story provides elements of the past (regressive) and imagined futures (progressive) of the authors. The culminating town hall and Call to Action allow the three characters to come together and connect "their complex, multi-dimensional interrelations" (Pinar, 1994, p. 26). Ultimately, the goal of the chapter is to practice the synthetical and "conceptualize the present situation" (Pinar, 1994, p. 27) to not only describe the current face of school choice but also share how to stand against it.

We hope that you can find an aspect of one of these characters that connects to you. We hope you can see the impact that school choice has on you. We hope that you join us in advocating for public schools and rallying against charter and voucher programs.

Town Hall for the Future: A Community Contends With School Choice

The hazy, early summer heat hung heavy in the evening air, its weight almost matching that of the James Elliot Gymnasium, whose aging bricks had long since blurred into the skyscape, awash with a twilight pink akin to the flush of happy youth—or diluted tragedy. Both backfiring engines with unmuffled motors, and flattening tires gently treading the cracking asphalt while crunching along, accompanied the energized chatter from a community coming together for the most anticipated community event in recent memory. From the younger children passing out flimsy cups of 25¢ lemonade to the wrinkled aunties frantically flapping their church fans as they bustled about conducting other folks' business, everyone who could be was there. Even those who couldn't be there were on their virtual way. Billy Jr. diligently walked Billy Sr. through how to Facetime Ms. Ernestine in the

STAND UP FOR PUBLIC SCHOOLS! STAND UP FOR STUDENTS!

THE TRUTH ABOUT SCHOOL CHOICE!
COMMUNITY TOWN HALL

WHEN: JUNE 21ST @ 7PM
WHERE: JAMES ELLIOT GYMNASIUM

JOIN US AS WE DISCUSS THE STATUS OF OUR SCHOOL, THE PROCESS AND IMPACT OF SCHOOL VOUCHERS, AND PROVIDE WAYS TO ADVOCATE FOR OUR EDUCATIONAL SYSTEM!

TOPICS IN OUR FIRST RALLY:
SCHOOL CHOICE,
THE INTENTION OF CHARTER SCHOOLS
SCHOOL VOUCHERS,
PUBLIC SCHOOL NEEDS
CREATING A 'CALL TO ACTION' PLAN'

nursing home. Or she would be hearing about it later from Mrs. Whistle, whose tight white curls held enough of those free, short pencils to ensure the accuracy of her receipts for the morning bus stop's opinion exchange.

Somehow, Some Way, They Did It

One of the town hall organizers was a student from the block who grew up to be one of the teachers in their community: Briana Matthews. Shuffled off to the side, trying to take up as little space as possible in the now standing-room-only sweatbox of a building, she subconsciously tore at her already frayed cuticles as the anticipation ran through her usually steady nerves in the face of all the people who could save her students' futures if she could get through to them and remember to breathe. She was about to get her fifth cup of lemonade when she was shocked after spotting one of the last folks she expected to be here, Raelynn, who waved in her direction while walking briskly across the room.

Instinctively, Briana lifted one of her stimming savaged hands in a return greeting, as the student Rolodex in her head fired up to explain which of her kiddos might have prompted Raelynn to seek her out—especially since, when last Briana had heard, Raelynn was taking advantage of being able to choose a different school. Wrapped up in fortifying herself for the unexpected social nicety, Briana luckily didn't initiate anything further as Raelynn passed right by to join a gaggle of other parents conversing together. Awkwardly trying to turn the aborted wave into checking the time, Briana's mixed face flushed when an empty wrist mocked her efforts, and she booked it to drown the embarrassment in another too-sweet lemonade.

Raelynn didn't notice Briana's dilemma. She was too focused on reintegrating with her fellow parents and repairing any connections she unintentionally severed from her past choices. Seeing tight smiles on some of the faces surrounding her, Raelynn subconsciously tightened her grip on her purse, whose straining seams held loose papers from research dives, a notebook filled with crossed-out names of officials she'd tried to contact with drafts of letters she stayed up late into the night writing, and pens whose grips, no doubt, are a tad crusted with some pesky crumbs from an emergency kid snack from long ago.

Deep in thought, she tried to justify her place here. She tried to support someone's soft-voiced descriptions of his fundraising efforts with public school vs. voucher per-pupil spending comparisons Raelynn can now recite in her sleep, when Karen got too defensive about signing the petition in support of defunding vouchers. Raelynn tried to prove she was there to support public schools, to prove her awareness of how school choice negatively impacts school systems, and to admit she was tricked by the false hope she was offered. Raelynn tried to do her part.

As a lull settled over the crowd, Raelynn looked around trying to scout how many people may be lurking who weren't actually supportive of saving their public schools... remembering how she was recently one of them. Once. But fresh from winning the battle against her ignorance, she was ready to fight and to wholeheartedly advocate for the public education she so believed in.

Speak it With Your Chest; Speak From Your Heart

Ms. Brown just found a spot to plant her roots when the gavel thundered in time with the heartbeat caught in her throat. Eagle-eyed, her fiery gaze immediately honed in on the official, as they hammered the crowd to order to begin what will no doubt be a meeting for the ages.

The official looked familiar, but Ms. Brown wasn't sure whether it was in the way like-minded folks feel familiar or whether she may have seen them at work during a family session during orientation. Normally, she tried to clear her thoughts of work when out of the office, but Ms. Brown had been finding it harder and harder lately when the middle schoolers on one of their college trips asked her why their school was shutting down and if that meant they can't go to college. Their expectant faces and the faces of all of the students who've sought refuge in her office over the years haunted her dreams while she wrestled with how to do her job when she was never trained to support students.

Everything Ms. Brown has learned came from her initiative and life experiences. Numerous awards on her walls and shelves spoke to the caliber of higher education professional she was. And yet, when she saw an email about this community town hall and the fate of the K–12 school district, one of her institution's partners, she was faced with how she wouldn't have any of those accolades without her students.

Understanding the importance of this school, Ms. Brown was compelled to learn more about their struggle, to express her concern for their students' futures, and to share reflections from her students who felt neglected and lost.

People who didn't know her well, may have mistaken her shaking leg as anxiousness, but just like the people here who assumed school choice is a good thing with vouchers and charters, they'd be wrong. For Ms. Brown's spine and soul were forged from the perseverance and struggle of her community; her blood was red from the fire in her veins kindled by her passion to bring about a more just world for those coming after her. Ms. Brown was not afraid. Ms. Brown wasn't uncertain. Not here. She couldn't contain the energy that empowered her to be a leader in this community even if she wanted to. She was ready to learn, and she was ready to get her hands dirty in the trenches with the people who brought them all together.

"Thank you for coming out tonight, everyone. Let's get started—we all know why we came today; we all know where we think we stand, who the opponents are, who our friends could possibly be . . . but what, personally, brought *you* here?"

They didn't know before: Now, they do.

They're ready.

As they lined up for a moment at the mic, Briana, Raelynn, and Ms. Brown all reflected on their unique journeys culminating in this moment.

Teaching the Teacher: Briana's Story

It was recess time, outside in the late summer or in the spring, at the tables underneath the lone shelter from the heat of the blacktop where other kids were playing games generally involving some type of bouncing ball or the muffled snicks of a jump rope. Being in 5th grade was already hard enough without the added stigmas of being fat, being a girl, and being in the "gifted" program—not to mention one who loved to read, watch anime, and was in the thick of a "say something" t-shirt phase. But I got by from learning who my people were—and we frequently escaped the outside exhibition of peak American childhood to find comfort in fantasy and the quiet.

This particular day, we had our notebooks and pencils; and I'll never forget how that purple, Papermate mechanical pencil with the magic, twistable eraser felt like a key away from my own brain noise. And it was this particular day that the girl I didn't know was going to become my best friend for 20 years and counting asked me to teach her how to draw.

This was the moment that made me an educator.

* * *

As I sit at my desk grading book reports, looking up occasionally to watch my own 5th graders make the most of indoor recess, I can't help but think about that day. Even though the weather and accompanying soundtrack were vastly different from the mild percussion of precipitation bouncing off the old, thin window glass and the dripping ceiling tile covered by the low din of chatter... there are a few students drawing together in the corner with their pencil stubs on the backs of old class papers, and I've never been so aware of all the years that have passed since I was them.

I never thought I would end up here; if you'd have asked my 5th grade self, I probably would have said I thought I'd be a voice actor or drawing manga, long been married, and raising my own children by now. But instead, I'm an English teacher who has to split their day between 5th/6th graders (and high schoolers because yet another colleague succumbed to the charter school plague), barely has time for two cats let alone a partner, and solely raising other folks' children because there just isn't enough of me to spare—though on particularly rough days when I'm nursing a whiskey green tea, curled up with my cats, and feeling sorry for myself, I'll look at the data for my neighborhood's school district and end up in tears thinking about my non-existent child being part of those despairing digits. Then the next morning, I can't look my colleagues in the eye with how mine are weighted to the floor from the heavy shame of temptation to jump from the public school ship with a voucher or via charters for some nebulous future... exactly like the TikTok parents we grouse about on the rare occasions we get our lunches and the even rarer occasions we can take them together.

Seems one of my most precocious students wrote about Dewey. It makes me want to punch my old desktop that hasn't been the same since he started being overloaded from the daily deluge of emails about our funding failures, how scores have suffered, the declining numbers—even thinking about how I named the desktop "Tom" after one of my favorite professors doesn't help to curb the fury that's tricking my eyes to think red ink spilt all over these papers... even though I don't ever grade with red ink, I'm not a monster.

The bell tolls and my kids start packing up their joys to march up and down the halls for whatever subject they have next—funnily enough, I think it's math; not that it matters with this being the last few days before summer.

I start gathering up my things to finish out the day at the high school when my teacher senses start tingling and I look up to see one of my artist students shuffling her feet. Not being able to see her freckled face clearly from the slightly frizzy curtain of her red-ish hair, I offer her a smile. But before I can say anything, she quickly hugs me, shoves a piece of paper into my hand, and then bolts out the door, carefully supporting her schoolbag whose remaining strap seems determined to not be one more thing to disappoint her like the wonky zipper and the hole from which she lost her favorite pencil.

Thanking whatever school supplies gods there are to not have been a paper cut victim, I carefully smooth out what looks to be her progress report from when I handed them out in homeroom earlier to avoid any report card surprises. Puzzled over why she'd give it back to me, the high As in English and Art amidst the low As and few Bs bring a smile to my face thinking about how far she's come since I was able to connect her parents with a friend of mine who didn't charge them for her ADHD testing.

Hearing Tom sounding off a belabored notification, I'm jolted from Rachel's gift to see the principal's "URGENT" email and habitually click it to skim quickly before getting on the road. Looks like that charter conversion is the solution the school board is thinking will be the best way to counteract our numbers nightmare; and the email is about all those figures, the funding offer, job opportunities for teachers to stay with the school, etc.

Not being in the mood to be inundated with this again, Tom's modem giving a grateful sigh after I pressed the power button prompts me to mentally note needing to write a thank you card as I start folding Rachel's paper... I notice there's something written on the back and undo my process to see a drawing of her holding my hand on a mountain of the books we read this year along with a hurried scrawl of "Dear Ms. M., Thank you for getting me to try Art class! I hope you're here next year! You're my favorite! Love, Rachel."

My body and mind completely freeze from the power of Rachel's gift and the epiphany of what the future might be for her, for all of my students. I think of the salaries that charter email listed, the promise of reduced workloads, the new and renovated buildings, the "unquestionable," "undoubtable" numbers improvement. I think of all the bills piling up on my counter, the costs of having children and owning a home, how I haven't had time to even think about a hobby.

I think about my best friend, my first Rachel, and the invitation to her gallery opening and how she'd be so proud of student-Rachel's lines.

I think of the whispers of discontent from my fellow teachers passing in the halls after school... and I think about how, once upon a time, I was at the March on Washington with the teachers who changed my life; and I think about when I had time for activist work.

I think it can't be a coincidence that these two Rachels converged the same day an email about our school's future arrived.

And as I rush out the door, I think about all of the people I need to call and all the work we need to do to save our public schools before it's too late.

A Parent Learns the Truth: Raelynn's Story

When my husband, toddler, and I moved to Ohio we were ecstatic about the prospect of being first-time homeowners. We'd lived a bit of a vagabond lifestyle previously—moving to a new city every few years and often changing houses yearly. Now that we had a child, it was time to settle down and Ohio was to be our home.

My husband and I had put a lot of thought into where we wanted to live. We had a specific style of home in mind, a strict price range, and a targeted community. Location was also important to us, desiring to be close to a freeway and live within a reasonable commute to work. We thought we had it all worked out until our realtor Kali said, "That neighborhood has a failing school district. I know you're new to the state and first-time home buyers. Why don't I suggest a few neighborhoods to you that are in good school districts?"

While we knew Kali had good intentions, we weren't overly concerned. "We come from one of the worst ranked schooling states in the United States!" I declared. "My wife is connected to many educators—she knows how to provide our children with quality education," my husband shared. We were both sold on the narrative of school choice. It didn't matter what school district that we lived in, both of us felt empowered to go out and identify quality educational experiences for our children. School choice was on our side!

Within a few months, we had closed on our home of choice and moved in. I had a home to call my own, a loving partner, a beautiful daughter, two excited dogs, and a neighborhood in which I felt I belonged. What more could I want? School was several years in the future and we could figure things out then.

I just didn't know.

* * *

When I think back to buying my first home two years ago, I still feel the excitement and stress of the experience. I also remember Kali's words, "That neighborhood has a failing school district..." I heard her at the time and quickly dismissed her warning, but once it started to directly impact my household, I became much more invested.

Last summer, the time came to enroll my daughter in Kindergarten. I felt all the feels.

How is my baby ready for school?

She's going to love going to school and being around new friends!

Monique loves to learn, I can't wait to see what they teach her!

Five is still so young, is she really ready to go?

Enthusiasm and fear jumbled together. And then another emotion hit me—anxiety. I went online to see what I needed to do to enroll my daughter in the neighborhood public school. I searched online for the school and the first thing that appeared were the reviews:

Don't send your kids here! Fighting, bullying, and incompetent teachers. Horrible experience...

Negative words filled the page. "Oh no!" I thought, "I should have listened to Kali."

After some more digging, I found that the school had been rated as failing for the past several years, and outcomes each year were worse than the year before. I knew that this was not a school that my child would attend. Immediately, I got to work exploring my options. After all, I felt it was my right as a parent to find the school that best fit my daughter's needs. I had several close friends who were educators, so I knew exactly where to look.

I started with the open enrollment policies for the neighboring districts. Fortunately, each district had enrollment options available. Unfortunately, information was not offered online, and you had to meet with an administrator in person to learn more. There were several charter schools in the area, so I explored their websites to learn what innovative teaching they offered and what made them unique. Because our home was located in a failing school district, my child qualified for a tuition voucher. I found a list of private schools that accepted vouchers and looked up their tuition rates. While the vouchers would help significantly, ultimately, I would still be responsible for a portion of the tuition.

While I appreciated the options school choice provided, I was also intimidated by the process. I questioned how parents without knowledge of the education system or parents with limited English proficiency navigate these complex and convoluted systems. Nonetheless, I pressed forward and chose a neighborhood charter school for my child. The building was beautiful, the teachers were friendly, the curriculum was STEM-focused, and the school boasted strong test scores.

I just didn't know.

* * *

"My daughter is on her final strike at school. If she breaks the conduct policy one more time she'll be kicked out. I know she needs to follow the rules, but Jasmine is hyperactive and needs a supportive, understanding environment. I wish they'd work with her more."

Stephanie, a mom from my daughter's soccer team, was sharing about her daughter's struggles in school. Jasmine attended the same charter school as my daughter. I was listening carefully, as my daughter had received her first strike last week.

Sonya jumped into the conversation, "Ugh, I'm jealous that you all have choices! Since we live out in the country, I don't have any reasonably close option in where my kids go. My tax dollars go toward your vouchers. Lucky you!" (Kaeser, 2023)

Vanessa chimed in, "Options don't always mean opportunities. My son goes to Sunny Circle Elementary School. We explored options in schooling but he has an IEP and none of the charter schools or private schools offered services that fit his needs. A couple of private schools even said they don't accept *students like him.* Are they really allowed to do that?!"

Vanessa went on to describe how even though her son attends a failing public school she knows that he's getting services to support his unique behavior and learning needs. She also shared her fear of him being kicked out of a charter or private school. In his public school, he has occasional outbursts, but staff are trained to de-escalate his behaviors and are understanding after the fact. Vanessa had heard too many stories where kids like her son were kicked out of private and charter schools and ended up behind academically due to constant school changes. While public schools aren't perfect, Vanessa felt assured that her son would have a consistent education experience and was not at risk of being expelled.

I was shocked at Vanessa's words. I had never heard this before. I had friends who taught at charter schools but when I stopped to think about it, none of them were special education teachers. When I asked about behavior support at my daughter's school, the response had been to follow their behavioral scripts and that they encouraged all children to behave in a standardized manner. Maybe her story had some truth to it.

I just didn't know.

That night, I looked into what Vanessa had shared. I was shocked. Charter schools and private schools were not held to the same standards as public schools. They have fewer measures of accountability through outcome reporting and teacher qualifications. They do not have to retain children the same way that public schools do and can expel students for a number of reasons, academically and behaviorally. While school choice claims it is for the benefit of students and parents, oftentimes students don't attain the same academic achievements as they would have in public schools. To add to the inequities, the state spends more per pupil on charter and voucher students compared to public school students. I had only ever heard school choice depicted in a positive way. I just didn't know the shadow truth behind it.

The next week at soccer, I started talking to Vanessa about what I had found. Vincent, another parent with a child on the team, overheard and joined us. Vincent began to tell us about a movement to expand the voucher program and he was upset about it. He was frustrated by constantly hearing about well-meaning parents being lured by the false promises of school choice while investors and corporations benefit from our lack of true awareness. Vincent shared with us that he was an advocate for public schools and had made it his personal mission to educate as many parents as possible. Like me, Vincent had been attracted to the concept of school choice. Unlike me, he learned the dangers while his children were still young and has been a public school advocate ever since.

Vincent shared the different ways he engaged in his public school advocacy work. He started simple, by talking to other parents. He used conversations like ours at soccer practice, chatting with his neighbors, and conversing with parents in line at the grocery store to share his passion for public schools and warn of the dangers of school choice. He attended school board meetings and asked how he could help. He joined a few organizations, such as Public Education Partners, and started a local school district advocacy group. He regularly engaged with elected officials to inform them of the dangers of school choice and the needs of public schools (Public Education Partners, n.d.).

Vincent shared how he also involved himself in public schools as a parent voice, to help support and inform school decisions. While he was involved in the parent-teacher association, Vincent also found ways to embed himself within the school system and recruit other parents to do the same. Previously, Vincent had served as the parent representative on the curriculum team. He's also served on review committees for potential programs and courses. Most recently, he was involved in the technology workgroup as a parent liaison. By staying involved, Vincent could provide a parent's perspective of the future of public education.

What really stood out to me was how Vincent responded when he spoke to parents who chose charter schools or used vouchers for their kids. He was patient and understanding. He spoke against the system, not the parents who enrolled their children in school choice programs. He actually made me feel better by explaining the targeted tactics school choice politicians and advocates use to appeal to parents.

"But my kid is already in a charter school, what can I do?" I asked after hearing all that Vincent had to share.

"Join me at our next advocacy group meeting," Vincent encouraged. "You'll find other parents in similar situations that you can form a community with."

Vincent went on to encourage me to give public schools a chance in the upcoming school year. He explained that switching schools mid-year would negatively impact my child and it also hurts the public school system. Funding is determined by enrollment at the beginning of the year, so funding for my child had already been provided to the charter school. Returning to public school would be placing another student into their classrooms without funding to support them.

I was hooked. I can't believe I just didn't know.

* * *

After the soccer practice conversation, I looked up the advocacy group that Vincent shared. I spoke with my spouse about all that I had learned and expressed my interest in joining. As we were talking, I realized how separated I felt. There is a fight for quality education taking place within our state and I unknowingly contributed to the issue by flagrantly avoiding public schools and shopping around for my school of choice. I needed to be connected to the issue and do my part to fight the school choice giant.

I began attending public school advocacy meetings. While I was nervous initially, the ease at which I connected to others in the group encouraged me to do more. I learned strategies for sharing information. I was provided with scripts for contacting my elected officials. I met parents who enrolled their children in the neighborhood public school and gained confidence about transferring my child the next academic year. Not only would my daughter have a group of friends established at the school, but I was more aware of the positive aspects of the school which outweighed the negative reviews that originally swayed me into school choice. More important, I knew I was doing my part as a democratic citizen by engaging in public education. The advocacy group provided me with tips for having these conversations with my daughter. Although she was only six, having discussions regarding public services for the public good is a lesson she was ready to learn.

In addition to monthly meetings, the group held events and workshops open to the public. While many of them were educational, some events were organized to fight for a cause. I found myself attending these events more frequently the more I engaged with the advocacy work. When I saw the town hall posting regarding the potential closure of James Elliot High, I knew I would be there. Not only would this closure impact my child's schooling in the future, but it also accentuated the school choice battle taking place. My opinion on school choice shifted after someone shared the truth with me. It was my turn to do the same.

I can no longer claim, "I just didn't know," and with that comes a responsibility I can't take lightly.

Hope and Higher Education: Ms. Brown's (Ms. B.'s!) Story

"I'm screwed, Ms. B. What are my options now?" My student's voice quivered as she stared at her computer screen. She has failed three courses this semester, and from what I could tell, the only band aid I could offer was a "Course Repeat," which would set her back a semester. Other students I advised echoed her same concerns. This particular student often spoke about how she was valedictorian in her school.

"It was *really easy*," I would overhear her say, "We barely did any work or would work on a single project throughout the year. I was a bit surprised, but I know I can get a 4.0 here, too. I mean, how hard could it be?"

Though most students were excited about their journey as first-year students in August, as the dust settled throughout the semester, many were surprised by the work required to do in their classes. Others complained about the fast pace of their classes and how they often felt behind and ashamed to ask for assistance. Many of my students came from charter and public schools, and often, their energy was depleted after weeks of class work. The conversation felt like a looped record. We saw a decline in our student's ability to stay on course with their work. Some decided to "take a break" from school, and we often did not see them again. Our Black student graduation rate decreased, and many named the culprit to be their previous school's fault. The lack of preparedness wore their esteem down. As the university tried to accommodate and provide what was not given to students to be successful, we also felt overwhelmed. If burnout was a contagion, we higher education practitioners needed a cure.

"We'll exhaust all possibilities, Hon," I replied, "You are not alone."

She shook her head and exhaled. We both smiled as we clicked on the university academic counseling page to explore the various ways to salvage her grade and get her to her goal of becoming a lawyer. The fan's wind made noise while our thoughts floated within the stale office air. I repeated in my head, "We can't lose any more of these students. I wished they'd known their options before they felt defeated."

* * *

My office window faced the entrance door, which meant many visitors would stop by and speak with me about anything that came to mind. I tried to make my office feel like a home, so I added pillows to the worn couch, area rugs, infusers, candy, etc., which invited students to sit and, after a few chews from their candy, open up about their day and the stress that often plagued their bodies. When discussing their career goals or academic journey, I used coaching tactics to help them become more acclimated with their new community and learn how to advocate for themselves when feeling defeated within their programs.

Our university had a tight relationship with the public schools in the area. The department I worked for hosted many mentoring opportunities, and we often visited surrounding public schools to work with some of their students. Many buildings were old, and though construction was being done on the streets, many schools needed renovations and drastic repairs. The overcrowded classrooms, matched with the over-exhausted teachers, would glare at us as we tried to engage with their populations. Sometimes, we crowd into their gymnasiums or cafeterias to play games with their students. Many of my student mentors tried to help with the high school student's reading and math homework. When it was time to go, we would wave goodbye and return to the van. The ride back was silent. Sometimes, I felt embarrassed passing out small swag items like candy or pens. These schools needed more than what we could give them. And now these students were my new college advisees.

Not all stories were the same, of course. I had some students who could maintain an excellent grade point average and were prominent student leaders. But, after the pandemic, we saw a decline in readiness and esteem from students who attended public or charter schools. I briefly believed in the words of our legislators, who, too, stated they were "disheartened" by the state of our education. "The answer is voucher systems," one article said, "give these students a chance to go to private schools! Use these vouchers to give them a great education and the pathway to success!" Shortly after, the governor approved a $2.5 billion dollar school budget to expand school vouchers and developmental services. The battle was then on for private, public, and charter schools to fight for that money. It was an unfair fight. And, though the smoking lights and mirrors was the amount of money being proposed, I realized that many people did not know how the voucher system worked and the damages it has done.

As I worked on another project, I heard my inbox chime. My eyes scanned the bold wording on the flier. Though I recognized the building in the background and the principal's name, what captured my attention was more than this familiar object.

The Truth About School Choice: Community Town Hall!

James Elliot High School was a school we worked with throughout the year. The email stated that James Elliot High was on the list of failing entities due to funding and grade reporting. Moreover, with the proper funding, they could stay put on the market to be made into a possible charter school. James Elliot was also often struggling for money. Though there has been an increase in the education budget, those familiar with its function were aware that these schools would rarely see it. As vouchers took money from the pot promised for public education, the primary receivers were private schools. So often, we receive these emails about public schools needing help. I couldn't ignore the call this time.

STAND UP FOR PUBLIC SCHOOLS! STAND UP FOR STUDENTS!

I wrote down the date and time of the town hall, motivated to be a part of this conversation. So many people don't know about this issue. The words "Stand up for public schools! Stand up for students" ignited inquiry within me. Perhaps it's not hopeless, but what can I do? I looked at the clock and quickly packed up stuff for my upcoming class. "Can I empower others to want to be a part of a movement that disrupts this? I wished my students knew their responsibility to lead this change. I wished they knew each other's relationship with this oppression." As I entered my classroom, I waved at my incoming students.

"What's on the docket today, Ms. B?" One student asked.

I smiled and clicked on the computer, "Oh, you know, schools, culture, and advocacy. Same ole, same ole."

* * *

I was an adjunct professor for a Culture and Engagement course which encouraged my students to reflect on their power and find a passion area that moved them to want to learn more. My students were college sophomores and juniors with diverse backgrounds and strengths. Though classes were twice a week, the cohort had grown close to each other and taken the time to learn about each other's lives. This week, I discussed cultural consciousness to prepare my students to theorize their experiences and observations in various research sites.

Many of my students majored in education, social work, psychology, and human development. Their assignment asked them to research and observe a site, and many chose charter and public schools around the area. I had seen a pattern within their papers which often reflected anger and sadness at the state of the institutions they studied. Many pieces outlined how teachers did not know how to control their classrooms. Others were surprised at the low reading levels and at the energy to *"just pass the kids"* even if they were not ready for the next grade. We focused many of our lessons on the issues within the educational system. I played a few news clips that interviewed students voicing their anger about the unsafe conditions of their schools. Then I explored the economics of the voucher systems to show the discrepancies between how schools are given resources or stripped of them.

The class sat quietly, but their expressions and posture informed me of their discomfort. The story was too familiar to many. Soon, a student raised her hand. She was a young Black woman who expressed her passion for student advocacy throughout my course. Yet, at this moment, she seemed unsettled. "I grew up in public schools. I remember I struggled with my grades, and I left so lost when coming to college" I could hear my student's voice begin to break as she held back her tears, "I know what school vouchers do to our community. My school struggled. I know many of my classmates couldn't even go to college. We lost confidence in ourselves. I just think that we deserved more. I just wish we would have known what the system was doing before it was too late."

Then she finally let her tears fall as a nearby peer rested their hand on her shoulder.

In a short time, my class began sharing their experiences and observations and exchanging questions and narratives. Their stories felt as if they were quilted together. They told stories of hardships with fitting into private schools, public schools being taken over by White business owners, etc. I thanked each student for sharing their story. I wanted to empower these students. I walked back toward the front of the class and reflected quietly on what I had witnessed. These students reflected the function of a democratic society that sought to inform and explore a variety of instruments that could bring attention to and challenge this oppression.

"Let me ask a question," I leaned on the podium to grab the class's attention again, "Are we powerless? We know there is a problem. We know that it's impacting the future generations. What can we do about it? How can we get the word out?" I watched my students' dispositions change slowly as they leaned more into my words. "I encourage you to reflect on these questions for a few minutes, and then I want you to talk with your group and exchange some ideas on how you can inform the community about school voucher systems or how you can bring attention to the experiences that are happening in these schools. How can you change the narrative?"

This time the students were more energized to talk about their action plans. After being able to share their stories, which were welcomed and embraced, I witnessed their demeanor change from being unsure of themselves to understanding their power and their responsibility. I overheard so many ideas formulated and heard feasible and informative ways that would bring attention to this oppression in the community.

"You know what would be cool? We could make a documentary or a social media campaign calling attention to the changes in our education systems," one student stated to her group.

"Yeah, or have a podcast. We could invite administrators or leaders who know about school vouchers to break down the economics and illustrate what it does to public school education," another student added.

"Elections are coming up, right? What about canvassing and registering our first-year students? We can even introduce the issues to them in a town hall style meeting."

"Oh! We can use the department as a registration post in October, right? Catch 'em as they come in? Can we, Ms. B?"

One by one, they spilled out more ways to impact their community. I smiled as I packed my items. I was excited to go to the town hall this evening. I wanted to share my experiences and follow in the footsteps of my students. I wanted to work with others to find a solution, too. I wanted to inform others who I wish knew about these continuingly painful stories caused by school vouchers. I walked towards my car with a different energy. I didn't feel defeated anymore. I felt empowered to do something. I wish more people had known about this oppression, so we could all work together to end it. I wish we all had known our responsibility to help others have equality and opportunities. But now that we know, we are responsible for informing those we wished would have known, too.

Passing the Mic: The Town Hall Rolls On

Thunderous applause of anticipation shook the hall from the electrified energy charging the air with heated fervor. Like chain lightning, it was devastatingly beautiful how each of the women's stories and journeys built upon the last one, serendipitously connecting the community together as they lit fires and shed light on so many things kept hidden from them in the name of profit. The women looked at each other, unable to contain the smiles slowly blooming across their faces knowing they were about to be heard and there was still hope for others to join their efforts.

Seeing the moderator's mirroring grin of triumph and nod to move forward with the town hall, with microphone in hand, Ms. B took a brief moment to gather herself amidst the still deafening cheers from the crowd. Her already straight posture tensed further as she stared across the swath of faces as if in a trance, trying to sort out her words to reflect on her experiences, and to recall the pain she had often seen within her students. As a person working in higher education, she knew her connection was more in the "aftermath" of it all with the students who chose to pursue college degrees. How could she fit within this narrative; and how could what she had to say be relevant? It was the students she supported who lived through the traumas of society and the schooling choices dictated by those outside the systems—she wasn't "directly involved." But for a split second, the audience's faces became the faces of her students and her shoulders stopped trying to convince her body to curl inward in uncertainty. Ms. B. knew her purpose, her reason for being there just like everyone else's. Their future depended on it. So, with a pointed clearing of her through to calm the room, Ms. B began:

> I am here to be empowered—and to empower our community. The beginning steps of empowerment are debunking the essence of vouchers, being informed about the painful reach of neoliberalism, and engaging in dialogue with those who have been victims of this oppression. I believe that I have demonstrated my desire to see the change that will benefit our future, while also understanding how uncomfortable it can be to feel vulnerable, to listen to others' pain, to assist with rebuilding our community. For far too long, I was just like so many of you. I believed I was powerless and didn't have the tools to make impactful changes…
>
> Though I still think about these things, I realize I can't make sustainable change without you, without all of us: the community. I want to be a part of the movement that seeks to create a democratic society, a movement that uses our voices as a collective instrument of disruption to all of the false promises many of us may have fallen victim to around vouchers, equality, and education…
>
> To the students who helped direct me: Thank you. It's because of their demonstration of what healing and accountability can look like that I can see the benefit of sharing our stories or even taking the time to understand the issues through the eyes of others. They reminded me how part of advocacy is the unwillingness to be complicit with the things which prevent us from inclusively progressing…
>
> As an educator, I'm consistently concerned with the livelihood of my students and how they'll overcome the issues which school vouchers and inadequate schooling may have caused. Yet I have hope in their strength and passion. I am committed to teaching my students the power of their voices and emphasizing the power of their vote. Thus, I commit to lending them

> my voice, to help the next generation grow and feel empowered. Humbly, I am open to this process...
>
> I do this for my current students, and those yet to come; and I wish we had known about this issue before it infested our country. But it's not too late; I'm ready to make a difference. This is our movement—our moment...
>
> We have time to restart this clock and to make our concerns known. These future students will be the next ones in this building and they'll be the ones asked to reflect on their stances and their power. If that's the case, I want to be a vessel of knowledge and introduce these issues early in my classroom and office. We are truly in this together; and we should be finding innovative ways to reach this new generation so they do not have the same struggle with this tragedy born from our own silence and ignorance...
>
> But now we know, and we must move forward to find a remedy. This is our Call to Action and our step toward a liberated society.

Ms. B. closed her eyes to bask in the roars from the crowd and to breathe in this moment of unity as it became part of her, as it joined the rest of the experiences that kept her standing strong for her students. Once centered again, Ms. B opened her eyes to look at Raelynn who stood just to the side and she extended her hand with the microphone to pass the spotlight for the parent of their trio to take the floor. With how the audience's cheers quieted from their anticipatory shifting in the uncomfortable wooden seats, it reminded Raelynn of her child and she thought of her family. This was more than personal for her. She envisioned her child growing before her eyes, praying they would always retain that sense of excitement, and how she wanted nothing but the best for them. But right now, in this space, she wanted to bring attention to what she had done, what she could still do, and what she needed help understanding so she could be better in order to protect the future of those she loved. Taking the microphone with a grateful smile to Ms. B., Raelynn bolstered herself to speak:

> I'm here to be an advocate for public education. The first step I took to demonstrate my support was to remove my child from the charter school they were originally attending and enrolling her in public schools this upcoming school year. I can't fight for public education with my words and support charter schools with my actions. And I'm sorry for not knowing that sooner...
>
> Thanks to the guidance of Vincent, a fellow parent, I have become involved in the James Elliot advocacy group. While I joined to do my part, I've been deeply rewarded by the connections formed with fellow advocates. They've taught me so much: How to contact elected officials; where to find statistics and information about school choice; and how to be brave and have tough

> conversations in order to support public education (Public Education Partners, n.d.)...
>
> I've also engaged in more passive forms of resistance. I volunteer at my child's public school—reduced funding results in stretched budgets, so extra hands are always welcome. Part of advocacy work is supporting what you DO believe in; and I believe in public schooling. I serve on the PTA, volunteer in the classroom—when my work schedule allows—and participate in fundraisers. More recently, I've been invited to serve on a curriculum team as the parent representative. I'm looking forward to exploring this new advocacy role. And when I'm unable to physically volunteer during the school day, I look for other opportunities to engage, such as donating supplies and helping prepare classroom activities. To be honest, it's rather fun to cut shapes from colored paper and I'm even happy to sort papers to help out the school's teachers (Kriegel, n.d.)...
>
> I am in awe of the wide community engaged in this work. Parents, educators, community members, young adults, retired folks... and students! Public education is a public good that impacts us all! We must remember the responsibility to support public education is not limited to parents and educators, but rather expands to all citizens (Stitzlein, 2017). We should all be prepared to stand up against school choice...
>
> If you're here today, it means you want to see the system change. If you're like me, once you learn the downsides of school choice, you aren't able to look the other way. Participate in a form of advocacy that works for you. We're all needed in this struggle. As democratic citizens, it is our responsibility to protect public education and to protect students.

Again, the rafters quaked from the community storm within. Raelynn just expressed that while they all have and will continue to have different journeys, all of those assembled can ignite the energy necessary to create accountability to each other and to commit to a plan regardless of whether they actively or passively continue in the movement. This time, when Raelynn walked towards Briana, it was intentional and she squeezed Briana's hand in solidarity as she passed the mic over to her. Feeling buoyed by her fellow speakers, Briana stepped forward and scanned the room, smiling when she recognized a lot of the people within the hall. Remembering them in her classrooms and even on the playground, she felt inspired to fight for her future while hearing her past so she could do the same for all her students past, present, and future. That sense of rightness that always comforts her in front of a classroom enveloped her as she began what may be the most important lesson of her career:

> I'm here today not just as Ms. Matthews who's taught so many of your children, but as Briana, too. I'm here to be inspired, and to learn how to be in a greater position of advocacy. I want to reconfirm my commitment to my

community and stay focused on eliminating these barriers no matter what may happen to my own career. It may seem like I'm just doing my job... but the reality is that it's hard. There are many days I question why I'm still here, like when my account's overdrawn from restocking our classroom library because the ceiling leak still hasn't been fixed; or when I'm asked to teach another class at another of our schools even though I haven't had time to prep or ever taught that grade...

I have friends work at private schools with fewer regulations, and supposedly lighter workloads. But when it's 11 p.m. after a long, hard day and I'm stuffing my face with ice cream contemplating giving into that private switch temptation... I remember the faces of the kids who need me—those who can't afford private education and may be left to fend for themselves; the children who charter schools expelled or excluded; the children who need the resources that public schools should be offering. Children, like I was, who *need* public schools. I stay committed to our school system for them...

I also encourage their loved ones to get involved. I invite them into the classrooms and talk to them more about this issue, when I can. Maybe this will raise awareness about school events or lack of resources impacting their child's experience. Perhaps I could do more to encourage them to stay informed about the services we offer... But we may never run if we don't take these seemingly smaller steps like sharing information and being transparent, being authentic, with where we stand. We all have to begin somewhere before it's too late...

This is where I stand: I stand with our schools and center the students in all I do...

So, though I don't really have free time, I find the time to write to my state legislative representative and give them a teacher's perspective. I let them know about the damage they're doing to public schools. I try to tell the stories of my fellow teachers and our suffering students so they can see the reality of their choices and put faces to those so-called failing numbers. There are real children, real people, behind this movement and they can't continue to hide from the inescapable consequences of their decisions. They need to know the names from those numbers, because this is personal and this is a problem we can fix...

I want to do more—it's why I'm here—to be among a community of folks who think similarly so we can tell our children stories with real "happily everafters" where people actually escape from towers because their community loves them enough to work together to take them apart; where dragons like those business executives behind the voucher-funded private schools have to go through all of us before they can hurt our precious children. Let's fight this school choice monster so all our students aren't victims of a poisoned apple voucher. These kids are our future and we have to protect them while we still can. Who's with us?!

Once the audience settled again after another galvanizing round of applause, for a moment, silence swallowed the space.

It was a silence of joy and a silence of anger. Anger from all the stories, the tales of pain and tragedy, the reflections of despair and desperation—echoes of defeat and lack of fulfillment. Yet, each account also brought visions of hope and power. It became evident that each person in this space wanted to work together to find a solution, but where does this community commitment truly begin? For these stories are not strange; they're sadly familiar songs many parents, observers, students, and educators have heard time and again. What we as a community must do, if we are committed to bringing attention to this issue, is to draft a call to action. Something we can always return to as we hold each other accountable, and to remember who we're doing the work for. Something born from exploring our commitment, our power, and our goals to fight these injustices.

It begins now.

Now we all know.

Now: we act.

A Call to Action

At the conclusion of the rally, the enthusiasm and motivation of the community members are high. They recognize the ease with which one can be swept away by emotion, only to see that energy fade if no direct commitment is made for change. The community members decide to not let this be the case. Public schools are too important. Action must be taken.

Written word holds power. Documenting intentions increases efficacy.

This Call to Action is the rally participants' documentation of how they will stand up for public education. They have something to vouch for.

* * *

We are called to this rally to set the tone for a movement that has long been ignored. Through anger and hope, we introduce this Call to Action to discuss school voucher systems and inequality in our school system while energizing and encouraging others to be a part of the change we need. Empowerment and advocacy have been evolving as we consider how to inform, impact, and involve the community in a collective action that will address that which binds and oppresses the body. We, as students, practitioners, parents, guardians, leaders, and advocates, invite the process to consciously and critically reflect on who we are, our power's influence, and how to align our movement with the growing needs of our students and children who will ultimately be asked to be a part of the revolution to change the world. As we have centered and named the oppression which binds us (neoliberalism) and its tenets (school vouchers, capitalizing of tragedy, economic prejudice, and racist institutions), we use this space to build and manifest a liberated arena. These sections will discuss the importance of being informed and informing our communities of this phenomenon, along with how to address these issues. Finally, we end with how to hold each other accountable and maintain the movement.

Empowerment: Informing and Addressing Oppression

For many, the first step to being an advocate and embracing their voice as an essential instrument for change is an uncomfortable process. All three women who stood on stage demonstrated this—from the quiet teacher to the complacent parent to the caring, higher education professional—yet all took a risk and shared their stories in a public way. This process means reflecting on our privileges, the things we have often purposely or unconsciously ignored, and the issues we may have gone out of our way not to understand or discuss because we were afraid to lose comfort. As advocates, it must be clear that our lives are tied to one another, meaning pain and victories are in some form shared. Neoliberalism seeks to insert a price tag on everybody, use capitalistic strategies to ensure educational profit, and, more important, continue colonizing and segregating, separating us as inferior and superior, enslaved and free. We must not buy into the school choice narrative. Collectively, we must commit to public education.

Advocating, however, invokes a power many may not know is possible. Empowerment is the understanding of an issue, the power to see hope and resolution, and the belief and desire to be part of the movement to achieve something better. In the reflection of school vouchers, many may see the dollar signs and become overwhelmed by how much is being used for schooling and the permanence of capitalism and racist logic within the educational system that prevents many marginalized institutions from avoiding an unfortunate pipeline. For example, Briana was overwhelmed, too. Even though she had a history of advocacy work and was a member of many marginalized groups, the demands of her teaching position took a toll on her and she felt powerless to do anything more than what she was already doing or choosing an ice cream flavor. However, she was reminded of the importance of continued advocacy when given a thoughtful student gift;

and was empowered to begin healing her systemic wounds little by little by building community and holding elected officials accountable to their own.

There are many ways to practice advocacy, ways that can foster long term gains from short term pains like a losing a little sleep to write to legislators, donating coffee money to local candidate campaign funds, volunteering to lead a book or school supplies drive for classrooms in need... Yes, it can seem daunting but the system wants everyone to believe change is impossible in order to keep the focus on the negative. Advocacy is a dynamic verb—not a static noun—and so there will always be ups and downs, ebbs and flows. Consequently, advocates will go through an array of emotions, but that's how we are healed, and thus believe that healing can be achieved.

Through this, healing is also community building, for what is a community but a symphony of many voices? We don't have to go about our work alone but rather we can surround ourselves with others who have critically examined the deceit thinking behind the voucher movement and choose to advocate for public education. We can heal collectively. Afterall, conversations at soccer practice and an appeal to become an advocate for public education from Vincent is what began the journey for transformation and healing, changing Raelynn's perspective and actions. Raelynn then formed a new community in her public school advocacy group. Look around you: Who is your community?

This voice is an essential instrument.

Without the voice, the world may not have grown into a new image, and we may have stayed stagnant while following harmful practices. It takes an empowered voice and body to bring attention to the issues while also using these voices to help theorize, (re)imagine, and (re)create something dynamically equal and beautiful.

Keep it Moving: Creating Community

Developing space for all voices to learn from one another while sharing informal and formal knowledge can fuel the beginning of this movement. These spaces may be in various settings, but the shared goal is to create an environment where all can learn and create a plan that brings change. Discussing public schools' current struggles to maintain good teachers or get resources needed for their students to be successful should be addressed. Or the discrimination that marginalized students experience within private schools because of their differences should be a focal point within these meetings. The center of this cycle is vouchers, and thus we must address its influence on our future.

Centering community, building trust among those impacted or a part of the voucher system process, and empathizing and supporting others creates spaces to have a dialogue to visualize what equality and liberty can look like for all. Yet, the voices of the oppressed such as those impacted must be heard to avoid the consequences of being recolonized. If not, we may be victims of the continuous cycle of Whiteness, neoliberalism, and the apartheid of opportunity.

Many have been exposed to tragedy. This tragedy can look different, but we can empathize while working through our stories to exchange remedies for what binds us. We acknowledge that sharing our stories, concerns, and dreams begins the process of unity. We also recognize that many in official offices may only share the smoke screen of facts. What is considered relevant to some are numbers. But the whole story must be exposed, which we believe is hidden and embedded within the narratives of those who have witnessed the destruction of education, have seen their communities navigate degrading conditions, or have been failed by schools or leaders.

The community must lead the movement because we, the people, are the most familiar with oppression. The oppression of the voucher movement does not solely rest on the shoulders of parents and children. It is an oppression of community rights—of children, young adults, childless households, families, and retired folks. We see this in each of our advocates. Briana, as a teacher, felt the oppression directly in her underfunded and overcrowded classroom. Ms. B., as a higher education practitioner, felt the oppression through the undergraduate and graduate students she mentored who felt underprepared for higher education. Raelynn, as a parent, felt the oppression of her child's educational opportunities. All are members of the community, all are familiar with the oppression school choice creates, and all are accountable as democratic citizens to support public education. Informing each other about how this oppression has presented itself in our lives begins the conversation. How has school choice impacted you? How will you share your experience?

Designing a Way Forward

In this town hall, we have addressed, called out, and confronted that which prevents healing. School voucher systems deplete finances, resources, and opportunities for future generations to transform and make the world equitable. Schools, founded to extend and create knowledge, have become mere businesses. And the voucher system, which was introduced as the golden ticket so all students were given access to a better education, has been used to label minority bodies while establishing legal segregation. Our movement addresses this while calling out those who benefit from this system to address it. A liberated society rests on the involvement of all; and must be designed by all.

Public, charter, and private schools should not be considered separate victims but all the same. Each entity has made strides to give students and the community a better life and education. Yet, vouchers pit one against the other. And because of this, each institution seems to have this burden they must deal with and a narrative forced on them. Some may say private schools are the answer to it all, but overlook how some may feel uneasy or unable to be authentic in this space. People like Raelynn, prior to her epiphany, will say charter schools have tried their best to provide positive experiences.

This is why the narrative created by those profiting from students must be exposed wide scale such as Ms. B's students sharing their stories and writing to their legislators. Even Briana wrote to her legislators about how public schools can be sites of inclusive education and freedom. However, they must remember to emphasize how vouchers strip them of resources and the inability to accommodate growing numbers or pay their teachers fairly. It begins with informing our community on the full array of issues. The painful experiences must be surfaced. And that is where we must be empowered to call out the source, to defend and assist all.

After we learn, acknowledge, and confront the dangers of the voucher movement, we must commit to taking action. Briana, Ms. B, and Raelynn were all complicit in the movement until they were informed of the dangers of school choice. Then they acted. Each found their place as advocates for public education. They became empowered to engage in advocacy work in ways best fitting their contexts and skillsets. They became accountable to the democratic right of public education. Now that you are informed and have identified your community, how will you design a plan to take action?

Building Elements of Accountability and Maintenance of a Movement

The community's and the movement's strength depend on the legacy left and the invested hearts captured. As we grow older, there may become a time when our knowledge and revolutionary tools are passed down and taught to young leaders. There must be a commitment for those who navigate as change agents, to always teach the younger generation who will have to learn how to disrupt the narrative of the oppressors and take an active part in creating something new and equal. This can begin at a young age—Raelynn had these conversations with her six years-old child—or start later in life. Ms. B encouraged her college students to take action. Moreover, we must be held accountable when committing to such changes. One block removed from the bottom of the foundation can destroy everything. This means the need to read, learn, discuss, and plan must be a continuous cycle when discussing achieving an anti-capitalistic approach within our education system. Additionally, we are forced then to depend on ourselves rather than politicians to make changes in our community or to be upfront and adamant about our needs and hold those in office accountable when things favor the dominant while neglecting the needs of the marginalized.

Accountability can come in various forms, depending on the person's action to challenge the prejudicial element. Yet, the one commitment is that we must all agree to liberate our present and future. For instance, in Ms. B.'s reflection, we witness her empowering her students and helping them understand that all people deserve adequate and safe education. Through this revelation, students also were encouraged to engage in actions that introduced this disparity to others while developing the narrative of equality. Their collective voice, in turn, echoes a sentiment of advocacy. More important, this action instills that all people deserve the right to have an opportunity towards success and access to the knowledge to make their world better. The student's commitment adds to the growing movement to speak truth and honesty while exposing that which keeps our communities disadvantaged and segregated.

That said, we acknowledge that victories may take time, and thus we revert to the importance of community. The journey of change can be tiring, and not one group can do it independently. As we grow into parents, grandparents, retired officials, etc., we must depend on the future generations' beliefs and energies to maintain the movement and bring attention to the issues at hand. Including students and young leaders in the conversation assists with the upkeep of the advocacy planning. We must present the issues to them so they can understand how this impacts their experiences and life.

Each generational wave has shown its ability and willingness to challenge injustice. Indeed, characters within this section have worked for or with various people representing these generations and have laid the foundation for them to ask challenging questions while seeking to rebuild and recreate a community that gives all children and educators a chance to be successful and free from neoliberalism. This movement depends on diverse strengths.

Without blueprints, they may not know (until it is too late) what lies ahead or recognize the inequality that depends on their ignorance and naivete. We all have a part to play in healing. This is the movement. The goal is to spread knowledge, reach out, engage in action, and create something that could change one heart and make others angry enough to be uncomfortable and want to see a change. So, it begins with the disruption of our logic.

To grow angry starts with information and understanding. To bring change begins with the space for all to imagine something different and pressure those in power to make a difference and not settle until all are liberated. And above all, we cannot rest in the momentary fulfillment. The movement must continue. The anger must remain. The conversation must go beyond these few pages. To heal, we must understand what is broken.

Now that you know, what will you do?

Taking responsibility means that in the face of barriers, we still have the capacity to invent our lives, to shape our destinies in ways that maximize our well-being.
—hooks, 2001, p. 57

Advocacy Action Items

There are various ways to get involved, advocate for equal education, and eradicate vouchers. Please use this checklist to create a plan that fits your style. Though this checklist is extensive, we know that some action items may not work with your journey—and that's okay! This checklist designed is to assist beginning and novice advocates in how to make an impact in their communities while encouraging them to reflect on how to use their voice and power.

Learn: Be Informed
- Read the statistics and decisions impacting the school districts around you
- Investigate how vouchers are created, decided on, and the impact they have on diverse demographics
- Explore literature from diverse resources such as blogs, lectures, pamphlets, governmental organizations, or non-profit research institutions
- Investigate how money is being spent in surrounding school districts
- Examine how vouchers have impacted similar states or communities
- Learn about the needs of surrounding schools by exploring their newsletters, investigating interviews given in articles, and/or by attending community meetings

- Identify the politicians who represent your community and investigate their interests, passions, and purposes. Do these interests align with justice, diversity, and equal opportunity?
- Explore and participate in avenues being currently used by local school districts, grassroots organizations, and/or community leaders who bring people together to discuss issues and take note of the various experiences being expressed

Reach Out: Build Community

- Talk to a neighbors, parents, and friends, etc. about what you've learned
- Ask others to share their stories with you
- Practice empathy and active listening
- Reflect on the stories shared with you and try not to compare or overpower the conversation with your experiences
- Promote an environment that invites challenge and support
- Ask uncomfortable questions and be ready for uncomfortable responses
- Share information on social media platforms (**PLEASE NOTE:** Verify all information before sharing with the community. Accurate information is essential to building trust and empowerment)
- Join an advocacy group for public education, such as Public Education Partners (https://publiceducationpartners.org/)
- Volunteer your time and/or resources to public schools
- Attend local school board meetings

Design: Brainstorm A Plan

- Set inclusive objectives that address the concerns and resolutions of diverse parties
- Determine what your "small victories" would be and make a guide to achieve these small goals
- Develop a list of contacts to send updates of any upcoming events or campaigns you may create and invite potential participants
- Create marketing (flyers, pamphlets, etc.) that details time, places, and any additional information needed for people to come and support the campaign
- Make social media posts that detail the issues and encourage others to repost or share this information with others
- If peaceful protest is your outlet, determine what items need to be available (signs, emergency items, etc.) and evaluate various protest routes

- Write to your local legislator
- Serve on a committee or task force within your public schools

GREAT WORK! Now how do you maintain it?

Manifesto

Have you seen the snowy flight of charter crows,
    a charismatic cacophony of company caws,
        fiscal filth feasting o'er our verdant fields,
            tear-salted from the poor bleeding red
                for the murder back in the black?

Coppers of the coffers—
    masked robber barons rubberbanding
    money to the market,
    barren to the many—
    reverse Robin Hoods
        holding foolish golden tickets,
    villains vouching
        for bespoke (broke) salvation.

Though with selfish arbitration comes hoarding precipitation—
    rife mirages, false pretension,
    distilled, dense droughts of dollar dissension—

Community destroyed from fright of white

in a realm ruled by the prophet profit—
    a predatory panopticon of pain and persecution
        choosing power
            over people.

But if we bring the thunder with downpours,
    if we expand, not expend, our public education—

Policy is a story ongoing:
    we can write anew, to pave new pages of public prosperity
    unchained and unyoked from private yields,
        where we the people are paramount,
        where success is not stolen by the so-called nonpareil,
        where empowerment is no longer exclusive.

Now: Here comes the rain.

References

Kaeser, S. (2023, June 5). Don't punish rural taxpayers by funding private schools they don't have | Opinion. *The Columbus Dispatch.* https://www.dispatch.com/story/opinion/columns/guest/2023/06/05/funding-ohios-public-schools-takes-priority-over-private-education/70279348007/

Kriegel, O. (n.d.). *How to best utilize parent volunteers in elementary school.* Western Governors University. https://www.wgu.edu/heyteach/article/how-to-best-utilize-parent-volunteers-in-elementary-school1709.html

Pinar, W. F. (1994). *Autobiography, politics, and sexuality: Essays in curriculum theory 1972–1992.* Peter Lang.

Public Education Partners (n.d.). *Get involved advocacy tools.* Public Education Partners. https://publiceducationpartners.org/get-involved/advocacy-tools/

Stitzlein, S. M. (2017). *American public education and the responsibility of its citizens: Supporting democracy in the age of accountability.* Oxford University Press.

EPILOGUE

A Peek at the Peak of our Pique

Thomas S. Poetter

I have to admit that it gets awfully bad, perhaps, when the professor quickly sidesteps to a three-homonym heading to provide a "soft landing" to our tale here. After all, we know from economic crises how difficult a soft landing is to achieve with so many moving parts floundering in the air as time seems to merely creep along. Such is the nature of a daily life in a democratic republic based on capitalism populated by a supposedly law-abiding, educated electorate. I really don't know what else to do with myself except to begin with word games to end this book given all that has happened in such a short period of time with the state of public education in Ohio.

Just recently a new universal voucher program was embedded in the state's new budget in Spring 2023, with the plans for it taking shape during our class May-June and with the details finalized just after we adjourned the class in late June 2023. It all feels like a blur, but not in a good way like you might feel after riding on a really thrilling roller coaster at a beautiful amusement park on a sunny, cool Ohio afternoon. More like you might feel when a ride like that gets stuck and the patrons are left dangling upside down dangerously for hours at a time. Bad scene.

But here I promise that I'll execute the set up to the end of this book with a glance (or a peek) at just how far we have we have traveled at breakneck (or peak) speed to an irritating end (pique).

One truth is that we have elected a supermajority in our state government that is hellbent on undermining/dismantling public education. In the past 6 months on the way to a new budget, the legislature funded a new universal voucher plan in an education budget that guarantees generous tuition vouchers and funding for charter enrollments to every family/child in Ohio. The funding is not tied to tiny escape hatch nods to "failing schools" as in the past, and barely protects the public from funding even rich citizens' private education dreams, now realities (the economic exclusion is 450% of the poverty level, or $135,000/year for a family of 4, but every family will receive some scholarship regardless of income; Shimp et al., 2023; Tebben, 2023).

And the legislature is hiding behind its decision to adopt a "backpack program" like this one where the taxpayers' money follows the individual child with its simultaneous pledge in the budget to fund the Fair School Funding Plan (FSFP) in Ohio, a six-phased plan meant to help public school districts achieve a fairer, more equitable funding scheme for public education that is less reliant on property tax. But that phase-in plan in six steps has only been guaranteed for the completion of the first four of those steps through 2025, and who is to say that the next nail in the coffin won't push the populace over to the non-democratic, systematic eradication of school boards, the elimination all together of audits of school expenditures (heaven forbid!), and/or the removal of safeguards to provide an adequate education at public expense for every student, etc., even if there is a modicum of fairness remaining?

But the fact remains that the state will be spending more per pupil on individual children in private high schools with its voucher program (@$8,407, $6165 for K–8 students) than it will for individual public school students across the state (@$7,300) (Tebben, 2023). That has been the case for nearly the entire life of the EdChoice "Scholarship" program (it's a voucher program) but it really hits home with the high figures coming at us in the new budget. And just think of all that could be done in our public schools to better our offerings, like providing complete services in all areas to all students, and educating each student with more opportunities than ever if we weren't sending more than $1 billion a year into private hands to be used in ways that none of us would ever approve of in public education or on the streets if more tax paying and voting citizens understood what was going on. Do citizens know that private schools and charter schools alike pay unqualified teachers, use public money to pay for the teaching of religious doctrine (talk about schools becoming doctrinaire!), and deliver students to the doors of charter/private schools on the public dollar every single day when many of those districts have drastically cut busing and when the football team at the public school, in many locales, has to find its own way to the Friday night game, no matter how far away the opponent?

I wonder what the reaction will be when the public school team plays the private school team across town this Fall in their annual games all over the state and the public school team arrives at the private school in 50 different cars all at the families' expenses of time and gas and wasted energy, increasing our dangerously high carbon footprint as a species and crimping already tight home budgets, and when the private school team arrives on a bus paid for at public expense for their playoff game with the same public school rival at the end of the season in a neutral site 50 miles away.

We might have to look at things on this level before we all wake up and say, "What?"

But for me, as a parent of public school children for many years and an advocate for funding and supporting public education and our students across the land in any ways that we can, my beef isn't mainly with this unethical, nearly legally indefensible set of facts and scenarios facing us all in Ohio and in several other states as we approach the brink of privatizing our education system. What troubles me the most is that there is a loss to all of us as the private education system gets stronger and stronger financially and politically when we make a decision that it doesn't matter that our children are going to parallel schools in common locales for reasons that are parochial, for religious reasons, and/or out of fear of others and their race or class or sexual orientation, and/or for fear of violence or of drugs or sex or crime, and/or out of hatred or distrust—any or all of it.

The further we get from each other, the less unified we become.

When the spaces we inhabit become fewer and farther between, we lose our identity and strength together.

This is hard to measure, but it is happening, and dismantling the public education system is an aspect of the issue that exacerbates the distance and peril that this movement of separating, segregating may continue to cause.

I understand that there are reasons that some students don't and maybe can't do well in public school settings under any circumstances. Nor am I saying that private education doesn't have its place—indeed, it may be the best option for some students. I myself have benefited from educational experiences in the private sphere. And I'm not saying that public schools are perfect; that has been made clear throughout this book. What I'm saying is that there is a societal and cultural cost to individuals and to us all as a people when we separate, when we make it possible for us to value the independent and individual desires as families and as persons over and above the common, the public, the good that serves us all.

The good that I am referring to here is the value that accrues to us all when we live and work and study together, not apart.

How do we make tough decisions later as citizens about our lives and the world when we don't know each other, and/or understand each other? When we don't care for each other, love each other?

Believe me, like most of you reading this, I have tried long distance relationships. They usually don't work. My bet is the further we are from each other over the next 50–75 years or so, the further apart we will become as a people, as a viable nation-state that is strong, hearty, united in friendship and kinship.

That's my fear: the distance, and the associated crumbling viability of relationships and understanding that define healthy communities, and the loss of vitality in a common set of purposes and vision for the future in which our talents and time are shared, not isolated away from each other in smaller and smaller dose and enclaves.

This is what I believe patriotism is: Fighting together for our community and communities and not just for ourselves.

Parochialism is a recipe for a lonely life, and valuing it more and more will probably create a weaker, more insular, and faltering civilization. It's not that aspects of our life that are parochial and private have no value, of course they do. But they don't define who we are and what we are to become. If so, our founders had it all wrong. I don't think they did.

I think these bedrock things are true in our given state affairs:

Commitments to accruing public funds and siphoning them into private hands, even legally, is undemocratic and ill-advised.

Scrambling for dollars dedicated to public causes and putting them to work for our supposed individual desires, needs, and/or projects is undemocratic and ill-advised.

Stealing from each other by separating our talents and lives onto different tracks out of fear, misunderstanding, hatred, and/or ignorance is undemocratic and ill-advised.

I want to close by saying three, final things.

First, greed and racism lie at the core of the voucher movement. Don't be fooled by the seemingly benign nods to freedom of choice and helping families fleeing supposedly weak, underachieving public schools. Choice is difficult to exercise except for the wealthiest of us and the public schools aren't weak, though they are underfunded and underappreciated. But they aren't weak. It's about money and fright/flight. Make no mistake about it and be honest. Remember, Ohio is the state that allowed the Electronic Classroom of Tomorrow (or ECOT), which reached an "enrollment" number of 15,000 at one point, to run a longtime attendance scam that yielded very few student attendees or graduates but resulted in a tremendous amount of revenue to the corporate entity and its executives. Its teachers and students were the predictable victims in a tragic case that "ended" in 2021. And the state has done very little to make sure that fraud of this kind is not repeatable (SchoolCEO, 2019).

Second, for years it has troubled me, no doubt far too much for my own good, that students left the public schools my boys attended K–12 for private schools or homeschooling. And it probably goes further back to boys I wished played on our eighth-grade basketball team in St. Marys but were still playing at for the local private, parochial school before finally joining us in high school. The people I knew who left our local schools for supposed greener pastures took their talents with them. I always thought of it as a form of theft, really, which may seem a bit harsh, but I heard one of my students say it this summer in class, too, independently of this long-held belief/feeling. When students leave and take their many potential contributions as talented human beings with them, it impoverishes those left behind who could benefit from studying and playing with them. It's a little sad to me, that is all of the potential for success and community alchemy lost when others leave, the promise of mutual benefit we accrue when we share our differences and become one. E pluribus unum, anyone? Anyone?

Third, citizen and school activist William Phillis of the Coalition for Equity and Adequacy of School Funding uses analogies of this type below to make his point about how ludicrous it is for public money to follow students to private schools. How long would citizens stand for an argument in front of a city council that John Tasker would like for the city government to fund his own private, backyard pool since his tax money goes to fund the city's maintenance and operation of the city's public pool which he doesn't use, for whatever reasons?

With a straight face, John says to the council, looking straight at the mayor, whose campaign yard signs he bought last Fall, "I pay my taxes like everyone else, and I like to swim, and others get a chance to swim in the city pool that I don't use (for whatever reasons among them being perhaps because it's too far away, or not deep enough, or doesn't have the right diving board, or doesn't have a baby pool, or it's not cleaned to John's standards, or certain neighbors use it that he doesn't like, or the swimming instructors use funny methods to teach swimming that he's not familiar with or doesn't believe in, etc). I would like to swim, too, but in my own backyard. So, I'm here asking that you allow me to use all of the tax money—and that of my neighbors who support me and our cause, along with a generous addition to our project out of the 'goodness of your hearts'—that is usually earmarked for the maintenance and operation of the city pool instead to build a pool to serve my neighbors and me privately in my own backyard to use and maintain and enjoy in perpetuity."

The Mayor responds, happily, "John, thanks for coming out tonight. We see your point, and would like to offer you $8,500 per year over the next four years to help you pay for this little project. We think that should build a nice, in-ground pool to share with just your close neighbors. And for good measure, we'll throw in long-term maintenance and transportation to and from your pool for your special friends you would like to include in your parties, and lessons, and whatnot, etc., over the next several years, as long as the pool is viable and filled with water. How does that sound?"

Maybe we should put private schools, and private libraries, and extra private parking, and pickleball courts, and pools, etc., in every taxpayer's backyard at public expense. Why not?

The answer is because paying for private education expenses out of public coffers in Ohio is unconstitutional, or at best illegal, at least unaffordable and unsustainable (Knight Abowitz & Malin, 2021). I think the same is true for swimming pools as well...

How long before a ballot issue in Ohio challenges the public's will to sink more than $1 Billion per year into private education enterprises, some of which are and will be corrupt and underperforming?

Perhaps only time will tell. What form of public, political activism are we willing to engage in together to challenge this movement, which puts us all in jeopardy?

To bring this book full circle from Chiquita's powerful preface, I want to ask these final questions: Is it possible that the rain that pours forth from interested and concerned people in Ohio and other states can act as a gentle, soothing rain of reason and possibility in the realms of public education and school finance? Does it really have to be the kind of pelting rain that comes along with a tornado, destroying, soaking everything in sight and bringing destruction? I say, let's rain, rain and as a result cleanse, irrigate, and grow. But let's stop the flooding, the casualties, the despair. None of it is necessary.

References

Knight Abowitz, K., & Malin, J. (2021). HB 290: A backpack full of empty promises. *The Capital Journal*. https://ohiocapitaljournal.com/2021/05/25/hb-290-a-backpack-full-of-empty-promises/

SchoolCEO. (2019). *ECOT: How America's largest cyberschool collapsed overnight—The electronic classroom of tomorrow's cautionary tale*. https://www.schoolceo.com/a/ecot-how-americas-largest-cyber-school-collapsed-overnight/

Shimp, D., Vorys, W., & O'Donnell T. (2023, July). *Client alert: Ohio legislature passes biennial budget; Governor Dewine approaches historic investment in public education*. DickinsonWright.com.

Tebben, S. (2023). Final Ohio education budget expands vouchers, limits board of ed powers. *Ohio Capital Journal*. https://ohiocapitaljournal.com/2023/07/04/final-ohio-education-budget-expands-vouchers-limits-board-of-ed-powers/

APPENDIX A

Class Reading List

Abrams S., & Koutsavlis, S. (2023). *Public Funds Public Schools Report: The fiscal consequences of private school vouchers.* Southern Poverty Law Center's Education Law Center. https://pfps.org/assets/uploads/SPLC_ELC_PFPS_2023Report_Final.pdf
Berkshire, J. (2021). Charter schools' scary future. *New Republic,* October, pp. 4–5.
Cowan, J. (2023). *School vouchers: There is no upside.* Albert Shanker Institute Blog: https://www.shankerinstitute.org/blog/school-vouchers-there-no-upside
Dyer, S., & Reedy, M. (2022, December). The promised education movement. *Columbus Bar Lawyer Quarterly,* pp. 30–36.
Golann, J. (2021). *Scripting the moves: Culture and control in a "no excuses" charter school.* Princeton University Press.
Hinh, I. (2023). *State policymakers should reject K–12 school voucher plans: Proposals would undermine public schools.* https://www.cbpp.org/research/state-budget-and-tax/state-policymakers-should-reject-k-12-school-voucher-plans
Lubienski, C., Brewer, T. J., & Malin, J. (2023). Bait and switch: How voucher advocates shift policy objectives. In K. Welner, G. Orfield, & L. Huerta

(Eds.), *The school voucher illusion: Exposing the pretense of equity* (pp. 127–147). Teachers College Press.

Mutch, C. (2018). It was like having the roots pulled out from underneath your feet: *Currere* and post-disaster school closures in New Zealand. *Currere Exchange Journal, 2*(1), pp. 40–52.

Perera, R. (2023). *State of the states: Governors and PK–12 education policy.* Brown Center Series by Brookings Institution Experts: https://www.brookings.edu/articles/state-of-the-states-governors-and-pk-12-education-policy

Phillis, W. (2022). Ohio Coalition for Equity and Adequacy of School Funding (Ohio E & A) Newsletter entitled "Papers of the Ohio Coalition for Equity and Adequacy of School Funding Regarding its Work on the DeRolph School Funding Case on File in the Mahn Center at Ohio University" (December 22, 2022 Edition: This newsletter edition along with many others from the Spring of 2023 constituted one of the reading packets for the course and students were encouraged to sign up to receive their own free subscription to the daily blog and newsletter posts by Mr. Phillis.).

Pinar, W. (1994). The currere method. In *Autobiography, politics, and sexuality: Essays in curriculum theory 1972–1992* (Vol. 2, pp. 19–27). Peter Lang.

Poetter, T. (2019). Life and death at Talawanda Ridge. *Currere Exchange Journal, 3*(1), pp. 105–113.

Poetter, T. S., & Googins, J. (2015). *Was someone mean to you today? The impact of standardization, corporatization, and high stakes testing on students, teachers, communities, schools, and democracy.* Van-Griner Publishing.

Resseger, J. (2023, April 18). *A Tsunami of private school tuition vouchers at public schools' expense: Is there anything we can do?* https://janresseger.wordpress.com/author/janresseger/

Sanders, R., Stovall, D., & White, T. (2018). *Twenty-first century Jim Crow schools: The impact of charters on public education.* Beacon Press.

Young, E., & Quinn, L. (2012). Defining policy advocacy. In *Making research evidence matter: A guide to policy advocacy in transition countries.* International Centre for Policy Advocacy: http://advocacyguide.icpolicyadvocacy.org=

About the Contributors

Abayomi Samuel Abodunrin is a doctoral student and research assistant in educational leadership, culture, and curriculum at Miami University, where he is interested in exploring the relationships between research, policy, and practice. Prior to his current role, Abayomi served as a public-school math teacher for almost a decade, gaining valuable experience in the classroom. In addition to his academic pursuits, Abayomi served as the Graduate Student Association Vice President at Miami University. He is a Fulbright Teaching Excellence and Achievements Alumni, completing the program in 2018.

Emmanuel Acheampong is a second-year doctoral student in the Educational Leadership Program at Miami University, and he is originally from Ghana, West Africa. He is a budding researcher, with his research interests revolving around issues in Education access, retention, and completion for underrepresented students, School leadership, and Teacher education as well as Education Financing. He currently has two publications to his credit.

Cerelia V. Bizzell is a PhD candidate in the Educational Leadership, Culture, and Curriculum program at Miami University, Oxford, OH. Her research interests include the experience of Black women working in Student Affairs, performance theory, racial surveillance, plantation politics, and segregation within schools. She hopes to continue writing works highlighting the disparities within marginalized communities and be a voice for those who often feel silenced and overlooked.

About the Contributors

Carolyn S. Craig is a PhD scholar in the Department of Educational Leadership at Miami University in Oxford, Ohio. Her research interests include the lived experiences of academic diversity officers in higher education; marginalized populations in STEM, healthcare, and business; diversity, equity, and inclusion in the workplace, women in leadership, and multicultural marketing. Craig is a Certified Diversity Professional, the inaugural Director of Diversity, Equity, Inclusion, and Belonging and a Visiting Faculty member for the College of Arts and Science at Miami University, and a former full-time business instructor at the university.

Mastano N. W. Dzimbiri is a PhD student in Educational Leadership, Culture, and Curriculum program at Miami University, Oxford, Ohio. His research focuses broadly on social justice education, social inequalities, politics of education, and geography curriculum/pedagogy in Malawi, Africa. Mastano's work draws on critical post-structuralist theory and decolonial approaches to better understand the existing social, cultural, and political hegemony in the production of knowledge and forms of oppression within the education spaces.

Tahreem Fatima is a PhD student in Educational Leadership with a concentration of Leadership, Curriculum, and Culture (LCC) at Miami University. She has a demonstrated history of working in the higher education industry with the aim to build teacher leadership in K–12 setting. Her research interests center around developing the concept of critical consciousness in teacher education and she is constantly seeking to understand the role the South Asian women contribute towards decolonizing education.

Chiquita M. Hughes is an educational consultant, children's book author, and doctoral student in Educational Leadership in the Department of Educational Leadership at Miami University. She has more than 24 years of experience in K–12 curriculum, instruction, assessment and professional development at the school, district, and state levels. Chiquita's scholarly interests include educational equity and advocacy, college and career readiness for underrepresented students, and engaging the voices of parents and families in educational spaces.

Elizabeth Rae Kerr is a PhD student in Educational Leadership and staff member at Miami University. Her research interested include instructional leadership, leadership development, and adult basic education. She has worked in various educational contexts including public schools, international programs, adult basic education, and higher education.

About the Contributors • 141

Dormetria Robinson Thompson is PhD scholar in educational leadership. Her research interests include Critical Race Feminism and the intersections of gender, race, the arts, and religion. With more than 20 years of experience as a K–8 educator, she currently serves as the Out of School Time Director at the Omega Community Development Corporation where she leads the Scholars of H.O.P.E. Afterschool Program and Children Defense Fund's Freedom Schools at two Dayton Public School sites.

Thomas S. Poetter, PhD, is a professor in the Department of Educational Leadership at Miami University, Oxford, Ohio; editor of the *Journal of Curriculum Theorizing* and *The Currere Exchange Journal*; and author of 65 journal articles and book chapters as well as 24 books, many of them in collaboration with student authors.

Shawnieka E. Pope is a PhD scholar in the Interdisciplinary Studies Doctoral Program at Miami University. She is a full time assistant clinical professor in Miami's Family Science and Social Work Department. Shawnieka has over 20 years of experience as a independently licensed and clinical social worker. Most of her career was serving K–12 scholars in an urban school setting. Her area of research is suicide in Black youth. Shawnieka is the proud mother of three adult children.

Dongxia Sang is a doctoral student in the Educational Leadership Program at Miami University. Her research interests include foreign language teaching and curriculum, educational policy analysis, and international student affairs. Before coming to Miami University, she was an educator in China for more than a decade. Also, she is a mother of two little girls who go to public schools in Oxford, Ohio.

Jacqlyn Schott is a Leadership, Culture, and Curriculum doctoral student and a Learning Specialist at Miami University. She plans to marry her passion for the arts and social justice by using arts-based methodologies to study radical care and transformational storytelling as tools for decolonization, achievement ideology, performance theory, crip theory, identity fluidity, and other epistemologies for developing critical, intentional pedagogy. As Jacqlyn's greatest desire is continued growth, she hopes to exchange knowledge outside of a traditional classroom, too, through theatre, Dungeons & Dragons, or any other creative adventure she explores.

Hope Porta Sweeney is a PhD student with a research focus in disability as diversity, culture and community. She is currently a disability Access Coordinator and Disability Studies instructor at Miami University in Ohio.

Jing Tan is a PhD candidate in the Educational Leadership, Culture, and Curriculum program at Miami University. Her research interests include language education, critical pedagogy, and educational policy analysis. She will join the Cincinnati Public Schools in the Fall of 2023 as a full time ESL teacher.

Tailyn Walborn is a PhD student in educational leadership with a research interest in public school finance, school choice, and how these perpetuate educational inequities. She is a higher educational professional with 10-years of experience working with students from diverse backgrounds, who share interests in STEM and healthcare career paths. While her professional passions focus on educational equity, she also enjoys baking, listening to records, and trivia.

www.ingramcontent.com/pod-product-compliance
Lightning Source LLC
Chambersburg PA
CBHW050638300426
44112CB00012B/1854